Let FORGIVENESS Set You FREE

A Step-by-Step Workbook for
**LETTING GO OF THE PAIN
& FINDING PEACE**

Meredith Hooke

Adams Media
New York • London • Toronto • Sydney • New Delhi

Aadamsmedia

Adams Media
An Imprint of Simon & Schuster, Inc.
57 Littlefield Street
Avon, Massachusetts 02322

First Adams Media trade paperback edition January 2021

ADAMS MEDIA and colophon are trademarks of Simon & Schuster.

For information about special discounts for bulk purchases, please contact Simon & Schuster Special Sales at 1-866-506-1949 or business@simonandschuster.com.

The Simon & Schuster Speakers Bureau can bring authors to your live event. For more information or to book an event contact the Simon & Schuster Speakers Bureau at 1-866-248-3049 or visit our website at www.simonspeakers.com.

Interior design, illustrations, and hand lettering by Priscilla Yuen

Manufactured in the United States of America

10 9 8 7 6 5 4 3 2 1

Library of Congress Cataloging-in-Publication Data
Names: Hooke, Meredith, author.
Title: Let forgiveness set you free / Meredith Hooke.
Description: Avon, Massachusetts: Adams Media, 2020.
Identifiers: LCCN 2020007975 | ISBN 9781507213513 (pb)
Subjects: LCSH: Forgiveness. | Self-help techniques.
Classification: LCC BF637.F67 H66 2020 | DDC 155.9/2--dc23
LC record available at https://lccn.loc.gov/2020007975

ISBN 978-1-5072-1351-3

DEDICATION

To my mother, Anne,
who has always believed in me.

CONTENTS

INTRODUCTION

Is there someone in your life you'd like to forgive? Someone who said something recently that hurt your feelings? Or who did something to anger you in the past—something you just can't let go of? Whether it's a friend, family member, partner, coworker, or even a stranger, there are times in every person's life where forgiveness is needed in order to move on from past hurt and flourish in the present. Just imagine how much happier you would be knowing how to quickly let things go—to brush off the little things in order to focus on the good in your life.

Of course, forgiving can feel easier said than done, and that is where *Let Forgiveness Set You Free* comes in. The exercises in this workbook have been laid out to provide you with a complete course on forgiveness. You'll start with an overview of why exactly you should forgive, followed by a few exercises to help you identify the benefits forgiveness will bring to your own life. Next, you'll take a look at what makes forgiving difficult and how you can navigate the common roadblocks to letting go. Later, you'll explore the role of control in forgiveness and what you are and are not able to control. Finally, as you move along toward your forgiving future, you'll touch on how to forgive when someone (including you) makes a mistake. But before you jump into the first chapter, be sure to review the following section on how to use this book—you'll gain insights into how to maximize the exercises in order to tap into your full forgiving potential.

As much as this workbook is going to teach you how to forgive other people, it's really about you. While we often focus on the compassion it takes to forgive others, we forget what a great act of self-compassion it is. When you know how to let these things go, you are free to enjoy the peace and happiness of a heart unburdened by resentment or anger. Once you've completed this workbook, both you and your relationships with others will be stronger, healthier, and more resilient. So, are you ready to forgive? Let's get started.

HOW TO USE THIS BOOK

While learning to forgive can feel daunting at times, this workbook is here to guide you through the journey to a more forgiving, and ultimately happier, you. In it, you'll find everything you need to identify and let go of the things that tether you to the past. Read on for more information about the chapters and exercises ahead, and how to get the most out of them.

Your Forgiveness Journey

Each chapter that follows will explore an important element of forgiveness so that when you have completed the exercises in the final chapter, you will have the tools to successfully navigate any difficult situation with a compassionate and forgiving mindset.

While many lessons can be gleaned within the workbook, there are three main themes that encompass your forgiveness journey ahead: the whys of forgiveness; the theories of forgiveness; and the cultivation of a more forgiving, happy you. These themes are described in more detail in the following sections.

Why?

As you set out on your journey to forgiveness, it needs to be clear to you why you're doing this. After all, sometimes you may question whether someone really deserves to be forgiven. You might even believe that holding on to a past hurt will protect you in the future. Chapter 1 will shed light on why it is crucial to forgive, and take you through exercises specifically designed to drive the message home. You will see how a lack of forgiveness has been robbing you of happiness and draining you of your energy, time, and focus.

Of course, even when you understand the ways forgiving will change your life for the better, there is still another pressing question: Why does it feel so hard to forgive? Chapter 2 is going to zero in on this question and provide a comprehensive look at why it's been difficult for you to let go of the past and move on in the present. The exercises in this chapter will help you pinpoint which common roadblocks get in your way, and give you the tools to overcome them.

The Theories of Forgiveness

The second part of your journey will be a deeper look into the three main theories of forgiveness:

- You Have the Power to Heal or Harm
- There's Only One Person You Can Control
- Everyone Is Doing the Best They Can

These theories have been developed over twenty years of intensive study and practice in ancient Eastern philosophies, as well as research in psychology and human connection. They are not faith-based teachings but a practical analysis of how the mind works and how you can unlock true happiness. When you understand the instincts and reactive habits people share, and the common patterns we all replay and become trapped in, you are able to rewire those instincts and habits to let go of pain and move on in peace.

You Have the Power to Heal or Harm

Just as another person's words or actions can lift you up or cause you pain, your own words and actions affect those around you. When you recognize this power, and choose healing over harm, you set the stage for forgiveness. You're more aware of the emotions of those around you—the stress they may feel, the pain or anger they may be carrying. And when faced with a rude comment or inconsiderate action, you can see the opportunity to heal through forgiveness, rather than lash out or build up resentment.

There's no substitute for firsthand experience, which is why the exercises in Chapter 3 will allow you to apply this theory in your daily life. In the first exercise, you'll practice "Random Acts of Forgiveness" that focus on taking a smaller step in forgiving by starting with situations that are less emotionally charged. Later, you'll bridge the practice of forgiveness to the feeling of connection with others, and you'll start to see the multiplier effects of forgiveness. When you experience just how good it feels to forgive through relieving others of their pain, you'll want to keep forgiving in the future.

There's Only One Person You Can Control

If only you could control what the people around you do and say... Wouldn't life be so much easier? Unfortunately, that's not the world we live in—but it doesn't stop us from instinctively trying to control others. After all, control is what makes us feel safe; if we can make others do or say what we want them to, we always know what is going to happen, so we are never caught off guard or unprepared. Of course, as experience shows, this control isn't a reality. It's an incredibly frustrating cycle and a guaranteed recipe for disappointment and strain on your relationships. Every time someone doesn't do or say what you expected or hoped, the resulting frustration or hurt makes it all the more difficult to forgive them. Instead, your grasp on that pain tightens as you replay the situation over and over, trying to figure out what you could have done differently to keep them from harming you. When you let go of that illusion of control, you can avoid this trap and create an environment for forgiveness and peace.

In Chapter 4, you'll bring this theory into your own experiences, beginning the exercises with a self-assessment of how controlling you've tried to be in the past. In "What Don't You Control?" you'll see how trying to control things you can't is a common thread that runs through many arguments you have with yourself and others. All the stories you have told yourself about why you're upset with someone will fall apart as you realize the role you have played in trying to control that person.

And while there are lots of exercises to help you give up control, there are also practices to help you refocus on what you *do* control. In "Responding versus Reacting," you'll learn to recognize reactive language, and how easily these words distort reality and set you up to feel and act defensively. You'll also explore the basics of how to set boundaries (in "Do You Need to Set Boundaries?" "Setting Your Boundaries," "When Larger Boundaries Are Needed," and "Saying Goodbye") to manage the time and energy you spend on people who habitually hurt you. While it's important to give up trying to control others, you do have control over who is a part of your life. By the end of the chapter, you'll take back the reins over the one thing you can control, cultivating greater peace of mind.

Everyone Is Doing the Best They Can

Everything you'll have learned from Chapters 1–4 will prep you to understand this final lesson in forgiveness. A common assumption when someone harms you is that they are not doing their best, that they aren't trying to do the right thing, or that they set out to be rude or mean to you. However, the reality is that behind biting comments and negative actions, there is someone else who's hurting, overwhelmed, or struggling in some way. Have you ever lashed out unintentionally at someone during a stressful moment? Or accidentally made things inconvenient for someone else while in a rush? Maybe you have managed to avoid these slipups, but the temptation was certainly there. When you step back and look at why someone might be behaving in an unkind way, what you'll find is there is almost always more to the story: Everyone is doing the best they can, and their best in one moment may be different (even hurtful) compared to their best in another moment.

Chapter 5 will explore this theory in more detail, with exercises that give you personal experience with its teachings to apply to your forgiveness journey moving forward. In "The Struggles of Others" and "Relate; Don't Hate," you'll practice looking at the possibilities of a situation rather than jumping to conclusions with limited information. In "It's Not Personal," "Flipping the Script," and "Has It Happened to Others?" you'll gain a firm basis for knowing when things aren't personal—and how to avoid taking them as such.

Later in the chapter, you'll practice self-compassion, understanding that you are also doing the best you can. When you see through the lens of compassion, there's no room for anger.

Continuing Your Journey with an Open Heart

There's a lot of information in this workbook. Not only are you getting rid of old thought patterns and habits; you are also taking on new ones, and it takes time for these to become your new defaults. Research from the Massachusetts Institute of Technology and Harvard University shows that reflection after learning something new improves your ability to retain that information. It is through reflection that you further embed these teachings into your mind and nervous system. This is why Part 3 of this workbook begins with reflecting on all that you've done and accomplished so far in your forgiveness journey. You'll tap into your senses to re-create different experiences and meditate on the emotions tied to each exercise.

Part of your continued journey beyond these pages will also be remembering what you need to do to maintain an open heart of forgiveness. To help you identify these next steps, you'll end Chapter 6 with a letter to your future self ("Dear Future You"). Here, you will look back on what exercises resonated most with you and what things you will need to remember—giving yourself a tangible keepsake to display where you will see it regularly.

Although the pages of this book will be complete at the end of Part 3, your journey will continue with each future practice in being a compassionate and forgiving person.

Your First Step

Now that you've taken a closer look at the different theories and exercises you will discover in the following chapters, it's time to begin. Start your journey to a more forgiving, and ultimately happier, you with the following self-assessment on how forgiving you are now.

HOW FORGIVING ARE YOU?

SELF-ASSESSMENT

Start your forgiveness journey by determining how forgiving you are right now. Here are several statements; give yourself a score of 1–5 based on how much each statement resonates with you.

> 5 = I agree very strongly with this statement
> 4 = I agree with this statement
> 3 = I somewhat agree with this statement
> 2 = I don't really agree with this statement
> 1 = I don't agree at all with this statement

1 If someone is late to meet you, you assume they don't value your time.

2 If someone interrupts you while you're talking, you immediately feel annoyed with them.

3 If someone disappoints you, it's hard to let it go and move on.

4 If someone has let you down, you're not sure how to address it in a calm and effective way.

5 If someone cuts you off while driving, you assume they are a jerk.

6 If someone doesn't call or text you back right away, you feel ignored and irritated.

7 When you do something for someone else, and they don't help you in return, you get angry with them.

8 If someone has an opinion that contradicts yours, you get defensive and think negatively toward that person.

Total Your Score: ☐

It's important to know where you are starting from so you can customize your forgiveness goals accordingly—and make the most of the exercises in this workbook. So, what's your forgiveness score? It will fall somewhere between 8 points and 40 points; the higher the number, the more you may struggle to forgive others. Remember: This is just the beginning of your journey, so don't be hard on yourself if the number is higher than you might have expected.

1
THE WHYS OF FORGIVENESS

Have you ever wondered if there was a point to forgiving? Or why letting go can often feel impossible? Maybe you've found yourself asking, "Why have I still not forgiven them after so much time has passed?" Forgiveness is something that many find difficult. Sometimes, a frustrating situation can even leave you wondering whether it is worth it. Does that person really deserve to be forgiven?

In the following chapters, you will explore each of these questions, along with why forgiveness is important and what common roadblocks may be keeping you from forgiving certain people in your life. Chapter 1 will help you uncover the price you've been paying for holding on to anger and hurt—the time spent focusing on the what-ifs, and the heaviness of these thoughts and emotions you are constantly carrying with you. Throughout the exercises, you'll see all the good that comes from forgiving, which marks the first step of your forgiveness journey. In Chapter 2, you'll discover the connection between forgiveness and stress, and the role stress has played in creating and maintaining conflict in your life. The exercises in this chapter will help you tap into a calm state in order to release harmful thoughts for good. It's time to embark on the first part of your forgiveness journey.

CHAPTER 1

WHY FORGIVE?

Forgiveness isn't just something that you are advised to do: It is actually good for you. Think of the weight of anger, resentment, and grief—all of the painful emotions that come with not forgiving someone who has hurt you. This burden moves with you from day to day, in ways you can notice and also in ways you might not initially be aware of. Maybe you feel on the verge of snapping for seemingly no reason, realizing only later that it stemmed from your lingering anger following a fight last week with someone you love.

When you finally forgive your friend for their hurtful words, you feel lighter. You put down the weight of resentment and move away from that emotion toward a place of healing and joy that radiates to every part of your life.

How Does Forgiveness Benefit My Relationships with Others?

Beyond the emotional release that comes from forgiving someone, it is also an important factor in maintaining healthy, happy relationships. In fact, many studies, including a 2011 analysis by psychologist Frank Fincham, show that couples who are forgiving are more satisfied in their relationships than those who tend not to forgive. Why? Because when you have a forgiving mindset, you see the whole picture, instead of focusing on the minor transgressions that inevitably happen from time to time. This view allows for the natural give-and-take of any relationship and helps you to keep your focus on the positives. And when times are tough, having these strong relationships to support you will make all the difference. Forgiveness also frees you. The promise of forgiveness means that your happiness is not dependent on what other people do; you may not be able to escape the challenges posed by others, but you can take away their power to upset you. This doesn't mean you allow them to walk all over you either. Sometimes you need to speak up and push back, and when it's over, walk away without holding on to any lingering resentment or anger. This is the kind of freedom that forgiveness provides you.

Sometimes, the need for forgiveness can come from a place of misunderstanding. How often have you misread a situation only later to find out you were completely wrong? It's likely that this number is greater than zero, and you aren't alone. Fortunately, the insights you gain through forgiving help you to tap into the possibilities behind why someone may be doing or saying a certain thing. By deciding to forgive them, you are putting yourself in their shoes and offering kindness where it might not come naturally.

How Does Forgiveness Benefit My Relationship with Myself?

As you explore the benefits of forgiveness in greater depth throughout the following exercises, you will also notice a common thread between them: personal values. Your values are what guide you in every decision you make and every relationship you have, including the one you have with yourself; they are your compass through life. And what you may not realize is that forgiveness is a part of these values. Healthy relationships, kindness, peace, and more all involve a forgiving mindset. You will uncover more about the connection between forgiveness and values as you complete the exercises in this chapter.

Why Does It Feel Difficult to Forgive?

Given how emotionally gratifying and enriching it is to forgive, you would think everyone would be practicing forgiveness all of the time. But as you know, it can feel challenging to truly forgive when you have been deeply affected by a situation. Instead, you can find yourself reliving the painful memory again and again in your mind—until you become stuck in a vicious cycle of thoughts that only make everything seem worse.

Where does this struggle come from? Survival instinct. Deeply ingrained in your genes are the impulses and intuitions that help you identify and avoid threats. After all, throughout most of evolutionary history, there were risks waiting at every turn. It was critical to take extra care to protect yourself by focusing on anyone (or anything) that hurt you. What if they tried to do it again? What if it was worse the next time? This is why negative thoughts are like Velcro: They were made to stick. So when you feel harmed, it can be tough to think of anything other than how this person has wronged you and how you can exact revenge.

What Now?

So what should you do when you feel those hurt, resentful emotions? What should you do when forgiveness feels out of reach? You may wonder where to begin, but fortunately there is a means of peeling away the Velcro of negative thinking, letting go of the pain you currently carry, and growing into a more forgiving, happy you—and it starts with understanding what harmful thoughts and feelings you tend to hold on to.

In the exercises in this chapter, you will learn specifically how *you* feel when you're unable to forgive. You'll also see how restrictive this mindset has been in other areas of your life, and how being more forgiving will improve your current relationships and happiness. As you uncover these insights into your habits and personal obstacles, you'll move one large step closer to true forgiveness. Let's dive in.

Losing What You Want to Lose

When you become a more forgiving person, you lose a lot—and that's a good thing, because in this case you are losing the negative thoughts and feelings that distort reality and make you unhappy. What things might you lose when you become a more forgiving person?

Instructions

Circle any of the following things that you feel you might lose along your forgiveness journey.

- Resentfulness
- Calmness
- Anger
- Relaxation
- Spitefulness
- Sympathy
- Isolation

- Confidence
- Bitterness
- Kindness
- Sadness
- Compassion
- Anxiety
- Wisdom

- Judgment
- Vengefulness
- Strength
- Tension
- Levelheadedness
- Irritation
- Hostility

Forgiveness Takeaway

Reflecting on what weights you might release along your forgiveness journey is a great way to cultivate personal goals for this workbook. Are any of these particularly heavy on your mind right now? These may be a focus of your journey; consider writing them out, with any further details, to keep as a reminder of what you are working toward in becoming more forgiving.

What Are You Focusing On?

Throughout evolutionary history, our instinct has been to focus on the negative. It may have been helpful in caveman times (surviving the many threats and navigating in a new world), but today, it causes a lot of anger and disappointment. When you focus your attention on the negatives, they overshadow everything else—building and building as you recount a past situation over and over. Eventually, you're consumed by them, unable to forgive what has happened and move on in the present. Taking back control begins with recognizing where your own attention is drawn.

Instructions

Here are some examples of common situations that involve both positive and negative responses. Imagine you are in each of these scenarios, and circle the response you would most likely fixate on.

1 You get a new haircut.
  a Friend A tells you it's a fashionable cut.
  b Friend B says it really suits you.
  c Friend C says it looked better before you cut it.

2 You need some help moving boxes into a new home.
  a Friend A is always or at least often available to help.
  b Friend B is super busy but tries to help when they can.
  c Friend C never helps or offers to help.

3 You give a lecture or presentation.
  a Person A says it was inspiring.
  b Person B disagrees with everything you said.
  c Person C says they relate to everything you said.

Continued on next page ▶

4 You have a new idea.

    a Friend A says it's a great idea.

    b Friend B encourages you to pursue the idea.

    c Friend C says it's a bad idea.

Forgiveness Takeaway

If you tended to focus on the negative response in each scenario, you aren't alone: It's a survival strategy that takes time and practice to break. Even if you didn't focus on the negatives in these examples, there may be situations in your life where you do, and this exercise is a great place to reflect on what kind of experiences might trip you up. Draw insights from your past: When have you focused on the negative before? Consider this as you move on to the next exercise.

Reclaiming Your Attention

Once you recognize when your thoughts are fixating on the negative, it's time to take back the reins and point your attention toward the positive. The following is a simple four-step mindfulness practice to help you disentangle yourself from harmful thoughts and look at them objectively in order to move forward with a forgiving mindset.

Instructions

Using the example of giving a presentation from the previous exercise, complete these steps. If you are currently dealing with a specific situation that has you focused on the negatives, use it in place of this example.

1 **Label the thought.** Identify what you're thinking about and label it. For example, "This is a thought that someone didn't like my presentation."

2 **Identify how you feel.** Think about how your body is feeling as you have this thought. Is your jaw tense or relaxed? Is there any sensation in your stomach?

3 **Consider, "Is it useful?"** Ask yourself if this thought is useful: Is it helping you in any way? Or is it more hurtful than beneficial?

4 **Breathe.** Take a few deep breaths in and out through your nose. Imagine each breath bringing your mind back to the present moment, anchoring you in the physical world.

Forgiveness Takeaway

This mindfulness practice uses steps that require deliberate movements and reflection to slow and ultimately quash those racing, negative thoughts. Now you can shift your attention to the positive, letting go of hurt feelings in order to move on in the present.

Measuring Energy Gains and Losses

Generally, you wouldn't think of something like regret or guilt as an activity, but it is. It requires a great deal of energy to keep these thoughts going. On the other hand, things like acceptance and hope can maintain or even elevate your energy levels. Each of these activities is a part of forgiveness—whether you are forgiving someone or holding on to hurt feelings.

Instructions

The following is a list of words. Using the lines provided, sort these words into two categories: those that give you energy, and those that take away some of your energy.

- Anger
- Kindness
- Guilt
- Resentment
- Hope
- Obsession
- Release
- Revenge
- Empathy
- Regret
- Acceptance

_____

_____

_____

Forgiveness Takeaway

Anger, guilt, resentment, obsession, revenge, and regret are all associated with not forgiving. And carrying these with you takes a lot of energy. When you're angry with someone, for example, the only way to keep that emotion going is to think about it, feeding its fire with your memories and pain. On the other hand, kindness, hope, release, empathy, and acceptance are all associated with giving forgiveness. As positive, uplifting emotions, they give energy to you. You will explore this theme more in the next exercise.

How Heavy Is Your Hurt?

When you hold on to past hurt, it becomes a weight that you carry with you everywhere you go. The first step in putting this weight down is seeing what exactly it is—and where it stems from.

Instructions

In the space that follows, draw the outline of a container: a suitcase, a backpack—anything you might use to carry things with you. Then fill that container with the names of anyone who has hurt you and who you haven't forgiven for that pain. If it's someone who has done multiple things that still weigh on you, write their name once for each time. Near these names, write the negative emotions they spark every time you think about them.

Forgiveness Takeaway

As you look over the different names and emotions you've written, can you feel their burden? Keep this weight in mind as you move on to the next exercise.

The Burden of Carrying Your Hurt

Bringing to light the different burdens you carry when you hold on to past pain is an important first step in laying down that weight. You recognize how heavy they have been and the release that will come from forgiving.

Instructions

Use your answers from the previous exercise to answer the following questions.

1　How full was your container?
   a　Overflowing
   b　Full
   c　Half-full
   d　Other: _____ (explain)

2　Now that you've taken the time to reflect, how often do you think you are carrying this weight?
   a　Most of the time
   b　Some of the time
   c　Not at all

Forgiveness Takeaway

You have the power to put these burdens on your back—and the power to set them down. But you'll only do this when you can see just how harmful it is to carry them with you. Keep your results from this exercise in mind as you move through the rest of this chapter. Later, you will uncover practices for setting down these burdens.

How Much Time Would You Get Back?

There is a calculable cost of not forgiving: time. And you might not realize just how much time is wasted thinking about the situations where others have angered, disappointed, or hurt you until you actually count it out.

Instructions

Spend one week recording every instance that you notice yourself thinking about a past hurtful situation. Note the frequency and length of those moments. Then use your record to answer the following questions on the lines provided. (You might want to have a calculator handy.)

1 How many minutes did you typically spend on average each day thinking about how someone had disappointed or hurt you? _____

2 How many days that week did you have these thoughts? _____

3 Multiply your answers to questions 1 and 2. _____ This is approximately how many minutes you typically spend per week focusing on those who have harmed you.

4 Multiply your answer to question 3 by 52. _____ This is approximately how many minutes you typically spend per year focusing on those who have harmed you.

5 Take your age and subtract 10. _____

6 Multiply your answers to questions 4 and 5. _____ This is approximately how many minutes you've spent in your life up until now focusing on those who have harmed you.

Continued on next page ▸

7 If you were given all of this time back, what would you do with it? Would you have spent it the same way, or would you do something else with that time?

_____

Forgiveness Takeaway

This is how much time you spend on negative thoughts and emotions. And it's time for the wastefulness to end. There are 1,440 minutes in each day. Why waste any of them on something that makes you feel unhappy? Consider how you might fill all this new space in your schedule: What activities and thoughts could you pursue to bring more joy into each new day going forward?

5:1 Interactions

According to relationship expert John Gottman, a ratio of 5:1 positive to negative interactions is important when maintaining healthy relationships. However, it is easy to focus on the negative interactions, forgetting everything good in the heat of a less-than-positive moment. A gratitude bowl can help keep positive interactions with loved ones firmly in your view.

Instructions

To create your gratitude bowl, you will need a few blank pieces of paper, a pen, and a medium-sized bowl.

1 Cut the paper horizontally into strips, roughly 2" wide.

2 At the end of each day, reflect on anything nice a partner, friend, or family member did for you that day. Maybe they called to check in on you, brought you a cup of coffee, put your dishes away, or picked up your dry cleaning.

3 Write these things down on the strips of paper, beginning each statement with "I'm so grateful." Then place the strips in the bowl.

Forgiveness Takeaway

The next time you are disappointed, frustrated, or upset with one of these people, pull out your gratitude bowl and start reading. Over time, it will become more of a habit to give your attention to the good things people do, so you can let go of those inevitable slipups.

Continued on next page ▶

Gratitude Bowl Bonus

After using your gratitude bowl for a month or two, it will likely be pretty full. Take out one half (or more) of the pieces of paper. Sort them based on the person involved in each situation, and place them into small gift boxes. Give the boxes to the people you wrote about to let them know how much you appreciate all of the nice things they've been doing for you.

Acknowledging the kindness of others is one of the most beautiful gifts you can give. It also opens up the conversation of how important it is for you to balance out positive and negative interactions to keep your relationships strong. With this goal in mind, you will be able to recognize when things feel imbalanced, and start a dialogue about what may need to happen to get things back on track. Maybe they need to forgive you for forgetting to do your part of the chores the previous day. Or perhaps you need to forgive them for pushing a joke too far. Together, you can tackle the challenge far better than struggling alone.

Becoming What You Want to Become

As you learned earlier in this chapter, forgiveness and personal values are intertwined. In this exercise, you will take a deeper look at this relationship by first determining your own values and then drawing connections to a forgiving mindset.

Instructions

From this list of common values, circle up to five that are the most important to you. Think about what things make you feel fulfilled and what things you look for in others: These may be key values in your life.

- Love
- Loyalty
- Commitment
- Open-Mindedness
- Generosity
- Honesty
- Humility
- Respect
- Courage

- Peace
- Happiness
- Harmony
- Balance
- Honor
- Joy
- Connection
- Patience
- Sincerity

- Integrity
- Wisdom
- Friendliness
- Empathy
- Maturity
- Credibility
- Strength
- Control

Forgiveness Takeaway

Many of the qualities of a forgiving mindset overlap with other important values that you may have circled. For example, kindness and open-mindedness are both qualities that are inherent in forgiveness. When you hold on to resentment and hurt following a situation where someone

Continued on next page ▶

has let you down, it is difficult to feel kind toward them in the future. They caused you pain, and you think of that pain every time you think of them. Forgiveness opens your heart, inviting more compassion in where negative thoughts and feelings once filled that space. Similarly, forgiveness helps you keep an open mind. In a forgiving mindset, you are intentionally seeking out new perspectives on a situation, considering the possibilities for why someone may have caused you harm, rather than jumping to the conclusion that they acted out of malice.

Keep these insights in mind as you move on to the next exercise.

Does a Lack of Forgiveness Compromise Your Values?

Although it may be hard to recognize or admit at first, the emotions and thoughts involved in not forgiving someone for a past transgression can have an impact on your values. For example, if one of your values is kindness, and one day you catch yourself delivering the perfect comeback to hurt someone who has criticized you, your actions aren't aligning with that value.

Instructions

Answer the following questions in the space provided to see how the emotions involved in not forgiving may be affecting your own values.

1 Have you ever spoken badly about someone who has hurt you behind their back?

---

2 Have you ever wanted to make someone you're upset with look foolish?

---

3 Have you ever wanted to make someone who has hurt you feel bad about themselves?

---

4 Have you ever said overly harsh words to someone who has hurt you?

Continued on next page ▶

5 Have you ever lied to avoid being around someone who has hurt you?

_____

6 Are any of these answers inconsistent with the values you circled in the previous exercise?

_____

Forgiveness Takeaway

When someone has caused you harm or disappointment, it can be instinctive to lash out or ruminate over your hurt. However, the negative thoughts and actions that are tied to not forgiving can also impact your personal values. Recognizing when your own behaviors are not in alignment with your values can be just the wake-up call needed to make a change.

Practicing Your Values

Now that you've explored the connections between forgiveness and values, and how a lack of forgiveness can contradict different values, let's apply these insights to your day-to-day life.

Instructions

Follow these steps to complete the exercise.

1 Before you set out for the day, review the values you circled in "Becoming What You Want to Become." Take a few moments to reflect on why these values are important to you, and how they connect to forgiveness:

_____

_____

2 As you go about your day, whenever you find yourself in a situation where you might be irritated with someone, reflect back to your values. Are your current thoughts and actions consistent with these values? If not, consider what needs to change to refocus on your values:

_____

_____

_____

_____

Forgiveness Takeaway

Sticking to your values is not always easy, particularly when you've been hurt. Acknowledging when your thoughts or actions are not aligned with your personal values is a simple way to refocus on the thoughts and actions that do align with your values. Considering how so many values overlap with the qualities of forgiveness, you'll be able to move toward a forgiving mindset by letting your values do the driving.

Peace Is Forgiveness: A Meditation

Something just feels off when you are in conflict with another person. It's a lurking sensation that things aren't quite right, and it keeps you from feeling at peace. As much as you may want to hold on to resentment or disappointment in the moment, you will continue to feel discontented until you let those feelings go. Remember: Peace is forgiveness.

Instructions

The following is a simple meditation on the connection between peace and forgiveness. You can do this exercise at any time to calm your mind and refocus on a forgiving mindset. Even better: It takes just a minute to complete, so you won't need to rearrange your schedule to incorporate it into your routine.

1 Sit in a comfortable position with your back straight. Close your eyes.

2 Slowly inhale and then exhale through your nose. As you inhale and exhale, silently say the phrase, "Peace is forgiveness."

3 Repeat step 2 for a total of one minute.

Forgiveness Takeaway

As you say the words, allow any thoughts or images related to their meaning to arise in your mind. By repeating the words slowly and reflecting on their meaning as you take deliberate, deep breaths, you embed this meaning into your nervous system.

Peace Is Forgiveness: Reflection Questions

This meditation is such a simple practice, and yet the words are very powerful: Every time you have had a conflict with another person and spent your time and energy dwelling on it, you move further away from peace.

Instructions

After completing the meditation in the previous exercise a few times, write down on the lines provided any thoughts that arose while you were saying the mantra "Peace is forgiveness." Also include any moments during the rest of the day in which you may have found yourself thinking this phrase.

_____

_____

_____

_____

_____

Forgiveness Takeaway

There is wisdom in these three simple words, as they are always pointing your thoughts in the direction of peace. They are telling you exactly what needs to happen to attain a content, forgiving mindset. The more you repeat them, the more their message will remain in the forefront of your mind as you move through your day.

Finding Your Reasons to Forgive

On your path to forgiveness, it's important to remind yourself of why you are working toward this goal. After all, even after completing the exercises in this chapter, there may be difficult situations in life that overshadow the lessons learned, leaving you wondering if it is really worth forgiving.

Instructions

Using the lessons you have learned from this chapter, fill in the blanks in the following statements with your goals for forgiveness and how you want it to impact your life.

1 If I were able to forgive more easily, it would improve my life by
_____.

2 My relationships would be _____ if I was more forgiving.

3 My values would line up with a forgiving mindset because
_____.

4 I would have more energy to put toward _____ if I could forgive.

5 I would be more _____ through the practice of forgiveness.

Forgiveness Takeaway

Mark this page to return to whenever you're feeling frustrated, angry, or disappointed with someone. Let your answers be a reminder of why you want to forgive—how it will feel to let go of that frustration, anger, or disappointment, and how your relationship with that person and others will be impacted through forgiveness.

Forgiving for Yourself

Sometimes, you may encounter a situation where it feels like the other person isn't deserving of forgiveness. Perhaps they really did act out of malice, or simply don't feel bad about hurting you. In these instances, it will be important to remember all the ways in which forgiveness is beneficial to you. While you may not believe they deserve to be forgiven, forgiveness is just as much for you as it is for the other person—sometimes more so. This will be your motivation to forgive in these situations.

Instructions

On the lines provided, create a list for yourself of the different ways forgiveness benefits you. Refer back to the previous exercises in this chapter for guidance.

_____

_____

_____

Now come up with a simple phrase that reminds you forgiveness is sometimes solely for yourself. This may be something like, "I am doing this for me," or "I forgive them so that I can heal." Write your phrase (or multiple phrases, if you prefer) on the line provided.

_____

Forgiveness Takeaway

Forgiveness isn't the same as reconciliation. You aren't saying you are okay with what the other person did. And sometimes, you aren't forgiving for their benefit at all. Keep this exercise in mind whenever you encounter someone you feel doesn't deserve forgiveness, and recite your mantra until you feel ready to forgive them.

Dear Past Self

Imagine a time when you were really upset with someone and held on to a lot of resentment as a result. Who were they? What did they do to hurt you? Once you have a clear image of the event in your mind, it is time to move on to the following exercise.

Instructions

On a separate piece of paper, write a letter to your past self. Explain why it's important for past you to let this situation go and move on. You can refer to different lessons from this chapter, or refer your past self to an exercise you found particularly helpful.

Forgiveness Takeaway

As you write, you may find there was residual anger from that experience—anger you can now release. Or you may discover the situation is similar to a current one you are struggling with. Let those words of wisdom sink in.

CHAPTER 2

WHY DOES LETTING GO FEEL SO HARD?

Letting go is one of the hardest parts of forgiveness. When you've been emotionally hurt by someone, a cut is made that is far deeper than any physical injury. The recovery is thus more challenging, regardless of whether the event happened two years ago or today. Maybe some apologies have even been exchanged, but you can't stop thinking about how that person harmed you.

Of course, others will be quick to say, "Just let it go!" but it's a lot easier said than done when your emotions have you bound to the experience. It's a helpless feeling—one that often leaves you blaming yourself. "Why can't I just let it go?" "It happened so long ago!" "They already said they were sorry": These are the common arguments many of us so often have with ourselves—arguments that only make us feel worse.

It's Not You—It's Stress

Before you start that blame game once more, consider this secret: There is nothing wrong with you for struggling to let something go; you are not the problem—stress is. Specifically, the mental and physical stress that arise in a threatening situation. Imagine you are standing face-to-face with a lion. There are no rails or glass panes between you, and the only protection you have are your own two hands. Thanks to evolution, your brain is programmed to respond to this situation by activating your stressed nervous system: Your heart rate and blood pressure increase, you receive a rush of adrenaline, and all available glucose goes to your large muscles in order to give you the best chance of survival. On top of this, you are on high alert, taking in every little movement and sound around you. It's the same response when someone emotionally hurts or disappoints you. Your brain believes that you are in just as much danger, and the same physical and mental responses are triggered—and continue to fire away every time you think back to that negative experience.

A key part of the mental response is self-talk. Your self-talk rate is anywhere between three hundred and one thousand words per minute, which works out to twelve thousand to sixty thousand thoughts per day. The more stressed you are, the more thoughts you have—and they aren't kind. According to the National Science Foundation, more than 80 percent of your thoughts are fear-based, and 95 percent of your thoughts are repetitive. You're rehashing the same things over and over—every disappointment, letdown, and insult that's ever happened: "They shouldn't have said that to me," "I should have gotten credit for that," "They are so inconsiderate," "How could they forget something so important?" With each repetition of these thoughts, your stress levels increase and your resentment builds.

Once you're in this state of negative thinking, you cannot see things objectively, because stress shuts down your prefrontal cortex (PFC). The PFC is the part of your brain responsible for logical and rational thinking, complex problem-solving, managing emotions, staying focused, and making decisions, as well as your working memory. You lose 10–15 IQ points when your PFC shuts down, and your caveman (survival-driven, instinct-based) brain takes over. This is how your thoughts become so wildly exaggerated, unconsciously refueling your resentment and anger over a situation that happened hours, days, even years ago. In your brain, lions are attacking. "Let it go!" Are they kidding? You could die!

This is a trap, of course, and in order to be more forgiving—to release all of the resentments you've been clinging to and stop creating new ones—you need to understand that stress is your biggest obstacle.

Your Next Step to Forgiveness

The exercises in this chapter are designed to help you tackle stress head-on, starting with the relationship between thoughts and stress. From there, you will learn how to rewire stressful thoughts to encourage more calm. It is only once your mind is at peace that you will be able to let go and forgive. Let's get started.

Words Matter

Some thoughts can send your mind into overdrive, encourage pessimistic feelings, and paint a negative picture of a situation. This is known as a state of stress. Other thoughts can slow down or even quash unhelpful self-talk, allow you to look at things from a different perspective, and put you in a more forgiving mindset. This is known as a state of calm.

Instructions

Write an "S" (for *stress*) or "C" (for *calm*) next to each of the following statements, depending on whether this thought puts you in a state of stress or calm.

1 They are so inconsiderate. ____

2 They must be really overwhelmed. ____

3 They might need a little space. ____

4 They are so rude. ____

5 They must be having a tough day. ____

6 They only think about themselves. ____

7 They must be under a lot of pressure. ____

8 They are so irresponsible. ____

9 They should never speak to me that way. ____

Now go back and circle which thoughts you feel are associated with a forgiving mindset. Do you notice a correlation between the letter you wrote next to phrases associated with a forgiving mindset? Answer on the following line.

_____

The phrases that are part of a forgiving mindset are 2, 3, 5, and 7. Do these match up to your answers? Answer on this line.

_____

Forgiveness Takeaway

Use this exercise to identify the common thoughts you may have that put you in a stressed state, and the forgiving thoughts (those you marked with a "C") you can replace them with to shift your state to one of calm.

Reframing the Situation

Think of a current situation that has you feeling reluctant to forgive someone. Maybe it's a friend who let you down recently, or a colleague you felt wasn't pulling their weight on a project you were working on together. Try to focus on an experience that isn't too emotionally charged but still a disappointment. Since you are just starting out, these types of situations will be easier to work with than those tied up in heavy feelings.

Instructions

Keep your chosen situation in mind as you answer the following questions.

1 Why are you angry at this person?

_____

2 How might you reframe the situation, using some of the calming phrases from the previous exercise? For example, maybe you were upset with a friend for canceling plans at the last minute with no explanation. Instead of assuming that they were being inconsiderate, what if you considered that maybe they were under a lot of pressure at home or work?

_____

_____

3 How do you see the situation now, after reframing it to allow for other possibilities?

_____

4 Do you feel more forgiving after reframing the situation?

_____

Forgiveness Takeaway

Reframing the situation doesn't mean you have to forgive that person just yet, but it does get you one step closer to forgiveness. When you reframe a situation, you are able to separate your initial thoughts and feelings from the reality at hand and explore different possibilities. Often, things aren't as personal as you may first assume.

You May Not Be Getting the Resolution You Think

When you're stuck in a stressful situation, there is an instinct to either run or fight. This was helpful in surviving during early human history. Today, however, that urge to protect yourself can cause you to cling more tightly to a negative experience and miss out on great opportunities in the future, for fear of being hurt again.

Instructions

Circle any of the statements that feel familiar when you've been hurt by someone, then answer the following questions.

- I will never help them again.
- I'll never put myself in that situation again.
- Doing the right thing always backfires on me.
- I'm done with them.
- I will never speak to them again.

1 What do you feel when you think these thoughts?

_____

_____

_____

2 Think back to past situations where you've had these type of thoughts: Have they protected you from future hurt, disappointment, or anger?

_____

_____

_____

3 Have these thoughts led to something positive later on?

_____

_____

_____

Forgiveness Takeaway

While you may not lash out directly in a hurtful situation, you have likely thought at least one of these things. They are tempting because they present themselves as protection: They seem to be looking out for your best interest, keeping you from harm in the future. In reality, all they do is allow you to hold more tightly to resentment, anger, and other negative emotions that make moving on all the more difficult. Use this exercise to draw attention to when these stressed thoughts creep in. Replace these thoughts with some of the forgiving statements from the first exercise in this chapter ("Words Matter").

The Power of the Pen

When you're upset, your thoughts move at the speed of light—eventually spinning out of your control. But while you think at a rate of three hundred to one thousand words per minute (closer to one thousand when stressed, anxious, or upset), you can only write about five to twenty words per minute. By writing down your thoughts, you slow them down, allowing you to see them more clearly and not get caught up in them.

Instructions

For this exercise, you will need a medium-sized bowl, a pen, and some pieces of blank paper cut into 2" strips.

1 Place the bowl, pen, and paper somewhere you'll see them regularly.

2 The next time you're frustrated or angry with another person, start writing out your thoughts on the pieces of paper (one thought per piece of paper).

3 After you've written down one thought, scrunch that piece of paper into a ball and put it in the bowl. Repeat this process until you've emptied all your upset thoughts into the bowl.

Forgiveness Takeaway

Training yourself to slow down your thoughts and gain clarity through writing them out is a vital part of your forgiveness journey. Your mind cleared, you will be able to address the root of your hurt feelings in an effective way so you can forgive the other person and move on.

Learning to Forgive Means Learning to Speak Up

Resentment can build up over time—without you even realizing it. It can often stem from little things people do that make you feel taken advantage of. Maybe a friend never offers to pay when you go out, or a colleague is always asking for you to help with their morning tasks because they are running late. Over time, these stressful thoughts begin to fester, keeping you from letting go and moving on.

Instructions

Answer the following questions about resentment on the lines provided.

1   Can you think of a time when little resentments built up to a bigger problem? What happened, and how did it turn out?

_____

_____

_____

2   Looking back, what might you have said before the resentment turned into a heavier stress in your life?

_____

_____

Forgiveness Takeaway

A big part of learning to forgive means learning how to speak up for yourself so those feelings of resentment can't build up in the first place. It takes just a few minutes to have a calm conversation with someone about something that's bothering you. You can even take some time beforehand to plan out what you are going to say to avoid blurting out something harmful or forgetting a main point you wanted to discuss.

Balancing Out Your Nervous System

In the first exercise of this chapter, you learned about states of stress and calm and the thoughts that spark them. Now you're going to look at the physical side of these states. Your emotions have a direct link to your body. For example, when you are scared, you may notice that your heart starts racing. Maybe your hands or legs shake or your chest feels tight. This is known as a stressed nervous system. A calm nervous system, on the other hand, involves a regular heart rate and steady breathing. It can also come with better focus and an increase in energy.

Instructions

For each of these mind states, decide whether it would put your nervous system into a condition of stress (S) or calm (C). Write "S" or "C" in the lines provided.

- Rational ____
- Clearheaded ____
- Angry ____
- Confident ____

- Composed ____
- Victimized ____
- Anxious ____
- Patient ____

- Afraid ____
- Disturbed ____

Thinking about each state and the options you chose for them, which nervous system makes you feel better? _____

Forgiveness Takeaway

These are all mind states associated with forgiveness. The positive mind states, such as clearheaded and composed, that calm your nervous system help you to forgive someone, as you are facing the situation with clarity and controlled emotions. On the other hand, the negative mind states (such as angry and anxious) that put stress on your nervous system only encourage hurt emotions, making it harder to forgive. In the next exercise, you will learn how to shift your nervous system from stressed to calm so you are better equipped to forgive and move on.

You're Safe: A Self-Compassion Meditation

A big part of balancing out your nervous system is to ensure you feel safe. When you are affected by an upsetting situation, you likely feel on guard and as though you are standing on unstable ground.

Instructions

One thing you can do to feel safe is the following simple meditation on self-compassion. It takes just one minute, and you can do it anywhere, anytime.

1 Sit in a comfortable position. You can either close your eyes or keep them open—whichever you prefer.

2 Take a slow, deep breath in through your nose, then back out through your nose. As you breathe, say the mantra "You're safe" in your head.

3 Repeat step 2 for a total of one minute. As you say the words, notice where you are: Is there a roof over your head? Do you feel comfortable? Is anyone hurting you?

Forgiveness Takeaway

When you do a self-compassion exercise, it's always important to use the second pronoun, "you," as though you are talking to someone else. Why? When you hear the words spoken this way, it feels as though someone with authority has come in to let you know you're safe, so you are better able to believe that you are. Once you feel safe, your nervous system will relax—calming your emotions with it—and you can evaluate the situation more clearly and confidently, setting the stage for forgiveness.

Learning to Slow Down

When you've been hurt, you move quickly. Historically, threats are something to get away from—fast. It's no different when someone has angered you: Your actions become faster and less intentional, and so do the thoughts racing through your mind. It is the stress response in full effect. In this exercise, you're going to get out of your head and back into the driver's seat by consciously slowing down your body's movements.

Instructions

Deliberately slow down the pace in whatever you're doing. Maybe you're making a cup of coffee: Take your time with each step as you fill the machine with water, change out the filter, etc. If you're drinking your coffee, slowly bring the cup to your mouth, take a sip, and then set it back down. As you walk somewhere, slow your speed. Feel your legs and arms moving, and your shoes connecting with the ground. When getting into your car, move slowly as you open the door and get in, carefully placing the key in the ignition to start the engine.

The first few moments may feel a little awkward, but as you keep moving slowly, being conscious of each move you make, you will start to feel calmer and less threatened. You are sending a subtle message to your brain that you're safe—if you weren't, you'd be moving faster.

Forgiveness Takeaway

Slowing down your movements puts your nervous system into a state of relaxation. In this state, you feel clearheaded and in control of your emotions, allowing you to address what you've been holding on to in an effective way. Now you are one step closer to forgiving what or who has caused you harm. You will also be able to brush off future disappointments and annoyances more quickly.

4-7-8 Breathing

When you're dealing with the heavy emotions of a hurtful experience, you tend to take short, shallow breaths out of your upper chest. This shallow breathing targets receptors that activate the sympathetic nervous system (stress response), telling your brain something is wrong. As a result, your brain is on high alert, making the situation feel even worse. Conversely, deep breaths in your lower lungs activates the receptors tied to your parasympathetic nervous system (rest response).

Instructions

Created by Dr. Andrew Weil, 4-7-8 breathing is an easy technique for tapping into the parasympathetic nervous system. You can practice it at any time, no matter where you are, using the following instructions.

1 Breathe in through your nose for four seconds, expanding your abdomen as you do.

2 Hold your breath for seven seconds.

3 Exhale through your mouth to the count of eight seconds, contracting your abdomen to push out all the air.

4 Repeat steps 1–3 four more times.

Reflection question: How do you feel after doing this exercise?

Forgiveness Takeaway

Your breath is powerful. Not only does it keep you alive, but it also regulates your mind, allowing you to slow down the thoughts and feelings surrounding a hurtful situation. In this relaxed state, you will gain the clarity to work through what has happened—and move on from it.

Physical Workouts for Forgiveness

When you've had an argument or someone's disappointed you, there is a really strong urge to do something, to act in some way. Remember, stress is a binary system: It is instinctive to either fight or flee. In order to effectively process and let go of your hurt, you will need to shift out of this stressed state and into one of calm.

Instructions

One easy way to release pent-up negative energy and become more relaxed is through physical activity. You can do one or more of the following simple exercises anytime you feel that stressed response coming on.

- **Air punches.** Pretend you're Rocky Balboa and punch the air with your fist for two minutes. Air punches mimic the fight part of the stress response, metabolizing stress hormones.
- **Running in place.** Just one minute of running in place releases tension and makes you feel calmer.
- **Push-ups.** Just doing ten push-ups can start to release some of that suppressed energy and help you feel more in control.
- **Dancing.** Put some music on and dance it out for a couple of minutes; not only will you release the stress hormones, but you'll also trigger the production of feel-good brain chemicals, including dopamine, serotonin, and oxytocin.

Forgiveness Takeaway

Every time someone angers or upsets you, these stress hormones are released. This exercise allows you to release them in a healthy way so you can shift back to a calm state. Once calm, you will be better equipped to process what happened and forgive the other person.

Loving-Kindness Meditation

During the stress response sparked by a hurtful situation, your thoughts race. You feel unsafe and maybe angry or confused, and your mind begins to create a story about the situation. The story starts with your memories of what happened and then builds out as you jump to conclusions about the other person's intentions, and worry about the future. As the story grows, so does your stress.

It's a cycle that can feel difficult to break out of; fortunately, a loving-kindness meditation can help you pull apart these stories and pave the way for a forgiving mindset.

In this meditation, you send loving and kind thoughts first to yourself, then to loved ones, and finally to a person you are struggling to forgive. The sequence is important: By starting out with yourself and your loved ones, you become more relaxed, open, and compassionate. By the time you get to the last person, you no longer see them through the lens of negative thoughts and emotions. The story you've told yourself about this person in the heat of the moment starts to fall apart; you understand that they want happiness and love just like you do. They have flaws and make mistakes just like you do.

Instructions

Follow these simple instructions to complete the meditation.

1   Find a comfortable place to sit where you won't be disturbed.

2   Play the guided meditation at www.zensmarts.com/loving-kindness-meditation and feel your resentful, angry thoughts melt away.

Continued on next page ▷

Forgiveness Takeaway

Doing this meditation doesn't mean you are forgiving this person immediately, but it does mean you are one step closer to forgiving them, as you are opening your heart and easing stress. In fact, a 2013 study by psychiatrist Helen Weng showed that just one day of loving-kindness meditation practice improved altruism and compassion in the participants.

After completing the meditation, look at how it has helped you feel more forgiving. Who was this person, and what did they do that you are holding on to? What kinds of thoughts were you having about them before the meditation? After the meditation, what thoughts do you now have about that person and the situation? As your negative story starts to fall apart, so do the emotions of resentment and anger tied to it.

Your Favorite Practices

The practices you did in this chapter are key in retraining your thoughts and rewiring your neural networks away from stress and toward calm. It is in a calm state of mind that you are then able to tackle tough situations in an openhearted and effective way.

Instructions

The following is a list of each exercise in this chapter. Rank them according to which ones you felt were most helpful in your personal forgiveness journey:

Words Matter
Reframing the Situation
You May Not Be Getting the Resolution You Think
The Power of the Pen
Learning to Forgive Means Learning to Speak Up
Balancing Out Your Nervous System
You're Safe: A Self-Compassion Meditation
Learning to Slow Down
4-7-8 Breathing
Physical Workouts for Forgiveness
Loving-Kindness Meditation

Forgiveness Takeaway

Spend some time here brainstorming which practices you can incorporate into your regular routine. What might your routine look like with these exercises scheduled into it? Consider adding these to your desktop or phone calendar so you'll remember to do them.

Stress Quiz

You've explored a lot of information in this chapter, learning how your thoughts about how others have harmed you spark a stressed response that makes forgiveness more difficult. Before continuing your journey in Part 2 of this workbook, let's reflect on the different insights you've uncovered in Chapter 2.

Instructions

Use the lessons you have learned from this chapter to answer the following questions.

1 A person has on average _____ thoughts per day.
   a 8,000–10,000
   b 12,000–60,000
   c 3,000–5,000

2 On average, more than _____ of all thoughts are negative or fear-based.
   a ½
   b ⅘
   c ⅔

3 The stress response shuts down the _____ of the brain.

4 The prefrontal cortex is responsible for (circle all that apply):
   a Rational and logical thinking
   b Complex problem-solving
   c Long-term memory
   d Managing my emotions
   e Motor function

5 When I am stressed, my IQ:

   a Increases by 10–15 points

   b Stays the same

   c Decreases by 10–15 points

6 Emotional symptoms of stress include (circle all that apply):

   a Compulsive behavior

   b Calmness

   c Irritability

   d Defensiveness

   e Compassion

   f Difficulty focusing

   g Increased memory recall

   h Anxiety

7 According to the National Science Foundation, 95 percent of all thoughts are repetitive. True or false? _____

Answer Key:

1 b	4 a, b, d	7 True
2 b	5 c	
3 Prefrontal cortex	6 a, c, d, f, h	

Forgiveness Takeaway

Stress plays a huge role in how you react to the things around you. Understanding this role, and using the tools in this chapter to reduce stress and manifest calm, allows you to process difficult situations effectively and with a forgiving mindset. Keep the lessons and activities from this chapter in mind as you move into Part 2 of this workbook.

2

THE THEORIES OF FORGIVENESS

The three theories of forgiveness aren't new. In some way or another, you have likely encountered one or more of these teachings in the past. Maybe you made a hurtful comment in the heat of an argument with a friend at school, later learning from a parent or mentor that you could have expressed your feelings just as effectively without harming the other person (You Have the Power to Heal or Harm). Perhaps you were upset one day because of changes being made at work, and a coworker reminded you that the situation was out of your control (There's Only One Person You Can Control). Or someone was rude to you at the coffee shop, and your partner responded that they were probably just having a bad day (Everyone Is Doing the Best They Can). In the moment, you may have found healing in these words, or, more likely, chosen to ignore them in your upset. And it is certainly easy to dismiss any idea when it feels abstract—an impersonal phrase thrown about in times of anger or disappointment. But there is so much more to these theories than nice words: each unlocks an important phase of becoming a more forgiving you.

In Part 2, you'll uncover the true potential of the three theories of forgiveness by exploring each in greater depth and connecting their teachings to your own personal experiences. Chapter 3 guides you through how to heal yourself and others, beginning with practices in less personal situations with strangers, before moving into more emotional situations with loved ones. Easing into the lesson of the chapter in this way will help you first process the theory itself, and then take a few smaller steps to practice it before tackling the experiences with those close to you that are often more challenging. Once you've made these intentional choices to heal rather than harm, you'll move on to the desire for control and how it is deeply rooted in our struggles with forgiveness. The exercises in Chapter 4 will help you let go of your own urges to control others and regain control over your own behaviors. Finally, you'll end Part 2 by looking through a new lens of seeing others as doing their best. You'll examine ways to shift your thoughts toward this perspective, and how choosing to give people the benefit of the doubt rather than judge them negatively is an important part of becoming more forgiving.

CHAPTER 3

YOU HAVE THE POWER TO HEAL OR HARM

Many of us know what it feels like to be on the other end of having hurt someone; whether it was intentional or not, the harm we cause becomes a part of us—and a part of them. While the memory of that pain is carried by the other person, it can also weigh on our own minds—in the form of guilt, negative self-talk, and more.

This is why forgiveness is a gift: By giving forgiveness to someone who has harmed you, you are making a conscious choice to relieve them of guilt and any other emotional weight created by a hurtful interaction between the two of you. It is your power: the ability to heal or harm.

Healing Proactively

Unfortunately, it can be hard to recognize forgiveness as the power that it is when it so often feels like something to be done only after the fact: You have to wait for harm to come your way, and once you've settled down your hurt emotions and had time to think about it, maybe you forgive the other person. This is the usual path forgiveness takes in our lives. However, it isn't the only one: There are actually countless ways for you to proactively heal through the gift of forgiveness.

Perhaps you notice someone who seems upset or stressed, and instead of passing them by without another thought, you consider that maybe they are feeling guilt you cannot see and extend forgiving vibes their way. Or maybe someone bumps into you on the sidewalk. Instead of reacting with an angry look or frustrated "Watch it!" you respond by letting them know that it's okay; it happens. Opportunities to forgive aren't restricted to major, emotionally charged situations—or even situations directly involving yourself. You can heal with forgiveness in so many ways.

What about Me?

Giving the gift of forgiveness is not only an act of healing for someone else. When you forgive others, you heal yourself too. Rather than carry the weight of anger, disappointment, or sadness from one situation into the rest of your day, week, or year (or even a number of years), you lay it down and move forward in positivity and optimism for the future. Even acts of forgiveness in less personal situations have a positive effect on your head, heart, and spirit. In fact, ample research shows that when you do something kind like forgiving another person, you get a boost of feel-good chemicals such as serotonin (which regulates anxiety, happiness, and mood), oxytocin (which is connected to feelings of love and connectedness), and dopamine (which aids in energy and motivation).

And emotional release and initial good feelings aren't the only ways forgiveness is a self-healing act. The following are other benefits to forgiveness that you will explore more in the exercises in this chapter.

A Shift in Focus

At one time or another, most people experience negative thoughts that are unhelpful. Remember: we evolved to focus on what could go wrong in order to survive. Whether you are worrying about a "what if" that is very unlikely and won't be answered for hours, days, or years, or recounting a situation that makes you feel regretful or embarrassed, harmful thoughts have a way of slipping into our minds every now and then. And once they take root, it can be difficult to let them go.

One great way to break out of these thoughts is through forgiveness. Proactively giving others forgiveness allows you to take your attention off yourself and redirect it toward someone else. After all, as many studies show, you can't give your full attention to two things at once; by consciously looking outward to other people and how you can relieve their pain through forgiveness, you are pulling your thoughts away from any negative self-talk and toward compassion and a positive mindset.

Connections with the World Around You

Choosing to heal rather than harm also helps you feel more connected to all of humanity. As social creatures, we need these connections in order to feel safe and content. In proactively giving forgiveness, you are increasing the number of positive interactions you have with others on a regular basis, establishing little connections that add up over time. This will grow into a stronger sense of connection with not just those people you've interacted with but also everyone in the world.

A Final Note about Self-Healing

Sometimes, others may not feel—or appear to feel—guilt for pain they have caused you. In these situations, it will be important for you to remember that giving forgiveness is not just about healing others but also healing yourself. Even if someone seems ungrateful for or undesiring of forgiveness, giving it will allow you to let go of that experience and move on in a kind, positive way.

Taking the First Step to Heal

The exercises in this chapter are designed to help you experience these benefits and more by providing easy ways to choose healing over harm in your daily life. At this point in your journey, you are still flexing your forgiveness muscles and strengthening the neural pathways in your brain toward a forgiving mindset, so the exercises that follow start with smaller steps. You'll begin by forgiving in a more impersonal way through your interactions with strangers. These situations tend to be less emotionally charged than those with people who are close to you, so they are a great practice in tuning into and managing the feelings you may have in a more personal situation.

Random Acts of Forgiveness

You may be familiar with random acts of kindness, where someone randomly does something nice for someone else. It's a beautiful gift that spreads a lot of joy. But what you might not already know is that you can go one step further and not only make someone feel good but also relieve stress with a random act of *forgiveness*. The anonymity of this exercise makes it easier for you to understand forgiveness more objectively, by removing the heavier emotions and pressure that are typically associated with forgiving.

Instructions

As you go about your day, actively look for opportunities to forgive people. When someone bumps into you, even if it is their fault, say as kindly as you can, "I'm sorry. I hope you're okay." As you say the words, also be sure to look them in the eye so they feel acknowledged.

If the waiter messes up your order or forgets your special request, let them know that it's okay: We all make mistakes.

If someone driving out of the parking lot comes a little too close for comfort, silently forgive them, instead of raising your arms and yelling. After all, it's a close call many have made—and is rarely intentional.

Forgiveness Takeaway

Be on the lookout for as many opportunities as you can to actively heal, relieving someone else's burden and filling your own heart with more positivity. You will use these experiences to complete the following exercise.

RAOF: Reflection Questions

After spending a day or more practicing "Random Acts of Forgiveness" (RAOF), let's take a few moments to reflect on your experiences in choosing healing over harm.

Instructions

Write your answers to the following questions on the lines provided.

1 What were the RAOF you performed?

_____

_____

_____

2 How did it feel knowing your response had the power to make someone feel better or worse?

_____

_____

3 Were some situations more difficult to forgive than others? If so, which ones?

_____

_____

4 Did any random acts you performed impact your overall mood that hour or day? If so, which act(s) and how?

_____

_____

Forgiveness Takeaway

Reflection after any intentional practice is an important part of processing what occurred and filing any insights or lessons gleaned from it into your long-term memory. In addition, when you reflect on how your gifts of forgiveness helped to relieve another person of pain, you trick your brain into thinking you're doing that practice again—giving you a second dose of those feel-good hormones and further embedding what you've learned and felt into your nervous system.

Acknowledging Healing Thoughts

As you learned in Chapter 2, 80 percent of your thoughts are fear-based by nature. The random acts of forgiveness you completed in the first exercise of this chapter work to alter this pattern by shifting more of your daily thoughts toward positivity. While you reflected on how these acts made you feel in the previous exercise, here you are going to reflect on how they made you *think*.

Instructions

On the following lines, write down some of the thoughts you had while practicing RAOF. Think back to the different acts and the mindset you were in as you gave forgiveness in each instance.

_____

_____

_____

Do you see a pattern in the type of thoughts you had during your random acts?

_____

_____

Forgiveness Takeaway

It's important to make the connection between the types of thoughts you're having and your forgiveness practices. As you give forgiveness in each situation, you recite compassionate, healing phrases that become a central part of your thoughts. The more these phrases are said throughout your day, the more they take root in your mind.

Bumping Into Difficult People

Among your many interactions with different people, not everyone is going to accept your gift of forgiveness as graciously as you might expect. In these instances, the resentment can start to build. "Why didn't they respond with kindness when I was so understanding?" "I shouldn't have forgiven them; they're a jerk!" These thoughts only lead to more resentment. In this exercise, you will stay the course to a forgiving mindset when people aren't as appreciative as you'd like.

Instructions

During your RAOF practices, note any instances of someone not appreciating your act or reacting to it in a negative way. After each experience, place your hand on your heart and begin saying the words "I forgive" in your head over and over until any temptation to feel resentful or angry with that person has evaporated.

If you are reflecting on a negative experience after a day of completing random acts of forgiveness, take the time now to ask whether resentful, angry feelings are still lingering. If they are, now place your hand over your heart and repeat the phrase as instructed.

Forgiveness Takeaway

When faced with a difficult person, that negative tendency you learned about in Chapter 2 is attempting to pull you down a path of hurt thoughts that only build until you are miserable. It is a path where you continuously harm yourself rather than heal and move forward. Through this exercise, you are creating a second path—one of positive intent—and guiding yourself down it. As you fill your mind with the decision to forgive, you leave little room for negativity to grow and instead allow your heart to heal.

Sending Out Forgiving Vibes

At one time or another, we've all had a selfish moment, acted impulsively, or unintentionally let someone down. It's only human!

In this exercise, you are going to give forgiveness anonymously. You will hold the person you are giving forgiveness to in your mind's eye and send them thoughts of forgiveness. Research by psychologists, including Dr. David Hamilton, shows that your brain doesn't know the difference between reality and imagination. Just imagining sending forgiveness to another person strengthens the neural networks of forgiveness in your brain. Similar to RAOF or placing your hand on your heart and saying the words "I forgive," you take a small step by healing someone in a less intense situation so you can practice having a forgiving mindset for a future situation that may be more emotionally charged.

Instructions

Write down the names of three people you know who might be in need of forgiveness. (For example, maybe one of your friends is having difficulties in their relationship with a family member. Or perhaps a coworker has seemed withdrawn lately after making a mistake on a company project.)

1 _____

2 _____

3 _____

Close your eyes and picture the first person in your mind's eye. Then silently say to them, "For anything that burdens you, know that you are forgiven. For anything that causes you shame, you are forgiven. For anything that causes you pain, you are forgiven."

As you say these words, imagine relief sweeping across their face. Savor the feeling of knowing you are welcoming peace into their life. Repeat this process for each remaining person.

Forgiveness Takeaway

Your imagination is powerful. In Chapter 2, you saw how your thoughts create stress, and now you're using your thoughts for something positive: healing someone else.

Waiting for Forgiveness

A lot of your life is spent waiting. Studies published by Priority Management Pittsburgh and other companies indicate that the average person will spend five years of their lifetime waiting in line, thirteen hours a year on hold with customer service, and nineteen full workdays stuck in traffic each year. Instead of letting it go to waste, you can use those times while you wait as an opportunity to practice forgiveness!

Instructions

The next time you are waiting for something—traffic, an open cash register, your morning coffee, anything—silently send forgiving thoughts to the people nearest you. They could be strangers or the group of friends or coworkers waiting with you.

As you bring your attention to each person, say the following in your head: "For anything that burdens you, know that you are forgiven. For anything that causes you shame, you are forgiven. For anything that causes you pain, you are forgiven."

You can also come up with your own forgiveness mantra, if you choose.

Forgiveness Takeaway

It takes no more than a minute to send healing thoughts of forgiveness to the people around you, and yet it has such an instantaneous effect on your outlook. Instead of being stressed or frustrated about the wait, you feel compassion, empathy, and forgiveness for all the people around you.

Reducing Harmful "Me" Thoughts

When you choose to heal through the gift of forgiveness, you also heal yourself. The negative "me" thoughts that drive defensive, impulsive, and unforgiving behaviors are redirected into a positive focus on someone else.

Instructions

Rate the following thoughts on a scale of 1–10, 1 being thoughts that make you feel terrible (stressed, upset, irritated, etc.) and 10 being thoughts that make you feel great (calm, compassionate, optimistic, etc.).

1 I've got so much to do; I'm so overwhelmed. _____

2 They must be dealing with a lot; I hope they're okay. _____

3 We've all said stupid things; I hope they don't feel bad. _____

4 He must think I'm so stupid. _____

5 Why does she always talk to me like that? _____

6 Something must be bothering them to act like that. _____

7 What if I don't get there in time? _____

8 They must be in a hurry; I hope they're all right. _____

9 Why haven't I gotten a text back yet? _____

10 They must be really busy right now. _____

Forgiveness Takeaway

The negative self-talk you play on repeat in your mind is a big part of why forgiveness can feel difficult—and why it's all the more important that you do choose healing intentions and actions. Not only do you relieve a part of someone else's emotional load, but you ease your own as well by redirecting harmful thoughts to positive ones. Use your results from this exercise in the following exercise.

"Me" Thoughts Reflection Questions

You may have noticed that the previous exercise had a pattern of thoughts that were "me" centered versus "they" centered:

"Me" thoughts: 1, 4, 5, 7, 9
"They" thoughts: 2, 3, 6, 8, 10

Total up your scores for the "me" thoughts and for the "they" thoughts:
"Me" thoughts _____
"They" thoughts _____

Instructions

The number of points accumulated in each category will fall within a range from 5 to 50. Use these scores to answer the following questions.

1 Which type of thoughts made you feel better?

_____

2 What kind of negative "me" thoughts have you found yourself ruminating over in the past?

_____

_____

3 Using the language of the "they" thoughts in the previous exercise, rewrite some of your own negative "me" thoughts to shift the focus onto "they" in a forgiving way.

_____

_____

_____

Forgiveness Takeaway

Not every thought about yourself is bad. Sometimes, however, a particularly difficult situation tempts you into a cycle of negative self-talk that fuels resentment, anger, hurt, and more. These are the types of "me" thoughts that harm everyone involved. When you feel those harmful thoughts bubble up, use the reworked "they" thoughts you created in this exercise to steer your attention in a positive direction.

Forgiveness Journal

As you discovered in Chapter 2, little irritations and resentments can often bubble just below the surface—even if apologies have already been made. Too often, we bottle these feelings up: "They'll go away eventually, right?" "I have too much to think about already!" At some point, the feelings find their way out—regardless of how convenient or inconvenient the timing may be.

Sometimes, as you learned in Chapter 2, you might need to speak up about these feelings. Other times, the right response is to let it go and move on. Try this practice first, and reflect on how it impacts the thought. As a general rule, if the same thought is coming up daily, even after doing this practice, it may indicate that you need to say something.

So how do you let go of these little irritations before they blow up? That is where this simple exercise comes in.

Instructions

At the end of each day for the next few days (or full week, if you prefer), check in with yourself. Did anything bother you that day? If so, write it down as though you've already forgiven it by using the reframing techniques in the second exercise of Chapter 2.

Examples:

- I forgive Sue for making that slightly off-color joke because I've probably done something similar in the past.
- I forgive my neighbor for blocking me in this morning because I know he may have a lot going on and just isn't thinking things through.
- I forgive Brad for taking the last cup of coffee and not refilling the pot because he was probably stressed out. When I'm stressed, I can act selfishly too.

Forgiveness Takeaway

Addressing little irritations at the start is important in keeping them from growing into something more challenging to forgive. As you write down each situation with a reframing phrase, you will be able to better let go of negative emotions and forgive what sparked them. With each phrase, you are also choosing to heal your own heart and manifest healing in the lives of others, rather than continue carrying hurt feelings.

Remembering How Forgiveness Makes You Feel

You've done a lot of forgiveness practices so far in your journey through this workbook. Every once in a while, it is important to pause and check in with your emotions.

Instructions

Take a moment to look at all of these words and circle the ones that describe how you have felt while doing these forgiveness practices. Feel free to write in your own options as well.

• Present	• Weak	• Frustrated	• Happy
• Bitter	• Wise	• Mindful	• Afraid
• Calm	• Stingy	• Courageous	• Helpful
• Peaceful	• Lonely	• Irritated	• Disappointed
• Kind	• Sad	• Angry	• Safe
• Fearful	• Supportive	• Energized	• Generous

Looking back over the words you circled, is there a pattern of positive or negative emotions?

_____

Are these emotions you would like to have on most days?

_____

Forgiveness Takeaway

Seeing how you have felt through practicing forgiveness in big words here is especially helpful in reminding you of why you are on this journey. Just as you have the power to heal others through the gift of forgiveness, you also have the power to heal yourself. Every forgiving moment holds positivity that lifts you up where the negative emotions of holding on would have weighed you down.

Forgiving Yourself As a Gift

You've seen how much healing it brings when you give forgiveness as a gift to someone else. Now it's time to heal through forgiving yourself. You get stressed, bump into people, and say or do the wrong thing occasionally—and you deserve to be forgiven for your mistakes just as much as everyone else.

Instructions

First, select a self-forgiving phrase (or multiple) that you can use to redirect your thoughts to compassion and understanding when you are being overly critical of yourself. Here are a few helpful phrases for different situations:

When You're Feeling Overwhelmed
- This is really tough, isn't it?
- Just a little bit more to go and then you can go home and relax.
- This is really challenging—you're doing great.
- You've gotten it done in the past; this time is no different—keep going.

When You've Made a Mistake
- That's okay: What can you learn from this?
- Everyone makes mistakes; let's look for a solution to right this.

When You've Been Short with Someone (after You've Apologized to That Person)
- It happens to the best of us.
- You've apologized to them; now it's time to forgive yourself.

Continued on next page ▶

You can adapt these phrases anyway you like, or create your own. Just be sure that kindness is at the core of the language you use.

Now, as you go about your day, notice when you are being harsh toward yourself. Accept that you are having an unkind thought, and then repeat your forgiving phrase(s), either out loud or silently in your mind in a soft, compassionate tone.

Forgiveness Takeaway

Learning to forgive yourself can feel challenging at first, but compassionate language directed toward yourself can ease the sting of a mistake or stressful situation and put things into a new perspective. Use the results of this exercise to complete the following exercise.

Forgiving Yourself As a Gift: Reflection Questions

After practicing giving forgiveness to yourself as a healing gift, let's take some time to reflect on your experience.

Instructions

Answer the following questions on the lines provided.

1 How did it feel the first time you recognized unforgiving thoughts toward yourself and then said a forgiving phrase?

_____

2 Did the number or intensity of unforgiving thoughts you had change over the course of the day?

_____

3 What phrases worked best for you?

_____

_____

Forgiveness Takeaway

Making mistakes is a part of life, and that's why having the tools to help you through these times is so critical. Forgiving language allows you to take control of your thoughts, guiding them toward healing rather than harm. Use the phrases that you felt helped the most in the previous exercise to redirect hurtful self-talk.

Forgiveness = Connection

Connections are a key part of the human experience. Unfortunately, busy schedules and modern technology make it easier to put authentic connections on the back burner. One of the many benefits of choosing to heal rather than harm is that you are making a positive connection with someone. You're acknowledging their struggles and letting them know it is okay; it is a profoundly deep bond when you recognize someone's pain and heal it through forgiveness.

Instructions

To become more familiar with how forgiveness manifests connection with others, you are going to again spend a day intentionally offering forgiveness to people. You can do so through any of the previous practices in this chapter, for example RAOF or more personal exchanges. This time, however, when you first see each opportunity for forgiveness, rate your connection to that other person between 1 and 5, 1 being not connected at all and 5 being very connected. Then complete the forgiveness practice. Now rate your connection to that person again. You can use the space here to record your ratings, take notes, and so on.

_____

_____

_____

_____

How did your ratings change after forgiving certain people? If any stayed the same, why do you think that was the case?

_____

_____

Forgiveness Takeaway

One of the core experiences in holding on to resentment or anger is a separation between you and other people. You may feel misunderstood or alone in your pain, or just want to isolate yourself from the world as the negative thoughts and emotions take over. Part of the healing that comes from giving forgiveness is bridging this gap: You release the feelings that keep others at bay, instead welcoming them in. This insight will help you stay the course when forgiving may feel more challenging or you may start to wonder if the effort is worth it.

Taking In the Goodness

After completing the previous exercises in healing, it's time to take a few moments to relive all the goodness your kindness has been creating. Psychologist and neuroscientist Dr. Rick Hanson has written extensively on the topic of savoring good deeds. He notes that when you relive the positive experiences in your mind, and connect your actions with the reward of feeling good, you strengthen that association in your motivation-reward pathway. In other words, the more ways you can relish in the experience, the more forgiveness will become second nature.

Instructions

The following is a simple meditation for taking in the good of your forgiveness practices. Read over the steps to acquaint yourself with them before completing the meditation.

1 Sit in a comfortable position with your back straight and close your eyes.

2 Take three deep breaths in and then out through your nose.

3 Now reflect on the different forgiveness practices you've done so far. Relive each moment as though it is happening right now: What did the moment look like? Sound like? How did you feel at the time?

4 Continue to breathe deeply as you relive the memories.

Forgiveness Takeaway

Savoring the goodness is a proactive way to rewire your brain to focus more on the positive than the negative. Every time you relive those moments of healing that you created for another person—and yourself—your brain thinks you're doing it right this minute. The neural networks that light up as you remember giving forgiveness become stronger, helping you build a positive habit that lasts.

What Seeds Are You Watering?

In each of us, there are a lot of different "seeds of potential." There are seeds for positive mind states like happiness, forgiveness, and contentment, and seeds for negative mind states like anger, resentment, revenge, regret, and disappointment. The seeds you water determine which mind state you nurture.

Instructions

In all of the exercises you've completed so far in this chapter (and the previous chapters of the workbook), you've been watering your seeds of forgiveness, filling your garden with happy mind states. Take a moment now to look back on the different exercises and reflect on the happy mind states you have watered with them.

Exercise	Mind State (e.g., calm, compassionate)

Continued on next page ▶

Forgiveness Takeaway

The analogy of all the different seeds of potential and which seeds you are watering is quite profound. It evokes a sense of power over your thoughts—that power to heal or harm—that many do not realize they have. Until taking the time to reflect through this imagery, you may not have realized how the intentional choices you have made through this chapter to heal have encouraged positive mind states that stay with you as you continue through your day. How do these mind states compare to those before you began your journey into healing over harming? Going forward, which seeds do you choose to continue (or begin) watering?

How You've Healed

You've done a lot of healing in this chapter, both in proactively looking to heal others and healing yourself. As you release more and more of your own hurt and manifest healing in the lives of others, you are opening your heart in a compassionate way. It is with this compassion that you take incredible steps in your forgiveness journey.

Instructions

Take a few moments to reflect on some of the important lessons from this chapter. Which practices helped you to heal your heart the most? Circle as many as you'd like.

- RAOF (Random Acts of Forgiveness)
- Acknowledging Healing Thoughts
- Bumping Into Difficult People
- Sending Out Forgiving Vibes
- Waiting for Forgiveness
- Reducing Harmful "Me" Thoughts
- Forgiveness Journal
- Remembering How Forgiveness Makes You Feel
- Forgiving Yourself As a Gift
- Forgiveness = Connection
- Taking In the Goodness
- What Seeds Are You Watering?

Continued on next page ▶

1 Going forward, which of these practices do you feel you could work into your regular routine to continue healing yourself and others?

_____

2 What would this routine look like with your healing practices included?

_____

_____

Forgiveness Takeaway

Reflecting on the practices that helped you the most, and how you can fit them into a regular schedule, will ensure you continue moving forward in forgiveness—no matter the situations you face down the road.

CHAPTER 4

THERE'S ONLY ONE PERSON YOU CAN CONTROL

"**I**f I had done certain things differently, they wouldn't have made those hurtful comments." "Maybe if I said something beforehand, I could have stopped them from doing that." When someone has hurt or disappointed you, it's tempting to turn to these what-ifs. What if you did this or said that? They wouldn't have upset you then…right? Maybe not—but maybe they still would have. The truth is that you can't control what someone else is going to say or do at any given moment. Yet so many of us so desperately try to. In fact, a 2010 study published in *Trends in Cognitive Science* showed that people are biologically wired to try to control their environment as a means of feeling safe.

This ingrained desire to control what others say or do also leads to expectations for how those people will behave. "If I express this, they will do that." "I know this is what should happen, so they will follow through." Whether you verbally express it or not, there is an implicit expectation on your side, and when the expectation isn't met, it often feels disappointing or even deeply upsetting. It's frustrating trying to control other people, and it takes a toll on both your relationships and your self-confidence. People are bound to do the unexpected, make mistakes, and disagree with one another on what is right from time to time. As individuals with unique experiences and values, you are not able to control them any more than they are able to control you.

Less Control, More Forgiveness

Learning to give up this desire for control is a huge step forward in becoming a more forgiving person. When you release your hold on another person's behavior, you also alleviate the hurt feelings that would have resulted from that person not doing what you had hoped or expected they would. Maybe it is still a bit disappointing that they didn't act as you wanted them to, but you were better prepared for this possibility—and understood it as being out of your control. Without those strong emotional ties to the situation, it is easier to forgive the other person and move on with a better focus on what you *can* control: yourself. It's an incredible relief, knowing that the only thing you have to worry about is how you react to the situations and people around you. Everyone else is responsible for themselves.

Breaking Past the Struggle for Control

In the exercises in this chapter, you're going to zero in on the things you don't have control over, and learn to break the habit of trying to control them. You'll explore ways to maintain your composure in upsetting situations so you can respond rationally and calmly instead of through heightened emotions. You'll also learn how to set boundaries and identify relationships that might be more harmful than beneficial. But before jumping into these practices in letting go of control, be sure to complete the self-assessment in the first exercise to determine how often and fiercely you try to control things right now. From there, you will be able to tailor your goals around control to your personal experiences.

How Strong Is Your Desire for Control?

Before you can let go of the desire for control, it's important to determine how much this desire plays into your life now.

Instructions

Following are some common situations that may irritate or frustrate you. On a scale of 1–5, how much do you agree with each statement? (1 meaning you don't agree at all, and 5 meaning you agree strongly.) Remember: Wanting to control things is a normal instinct, so be honest in your answers.

1   If I've asked someone to do something and they don't do it the way I wanted them to, I get irritated. _____

2   If someone says they're going to meet me at a certain time and they don't, I get angry. _____

3   If my partner says they'll take out the trash and they don't do it when I expected them to, I get upset. _____

4   If someone doesn't respond to my good news with the right amount of enthusiasm, I feel upset with them. _____

5   If someone asks for my advice but doesn't follow it, I get frustrated with them. _____

6   If someone breaks a rule, like parking in a handicapped spot when they are clearly not handicapped, it bothers me. _____

Total up your score: _____

Continued on next page ▶

Forgiveness Takeaway

Your score will fall between 6 and 30 points; the higher your score is, the stronger your drive to control the situations and people around you. To some degree or another, many people desire control, and sometimes your own controlling behaviors may surprise you. Keep this score in mind as you move through the following exercises: It will be the basis of your own goals surrounding control. In the next exercise, you will explore which situations are not within your control.

What Don't You Control?

Now that you have identified how strong your desire for control is, let's take a look at what things you cannot control—as much as you might want to.

Instructions

The following are everyday situations each of us experience in our life. Consider each situation: Are you able to control it? Circle the situations you are not able to give a "yes" answer to.

- Other People's Moods
- My Mood
- The Weather
- Unexpected Computer Issues
- What I Say
- Being Stuck in Traffic
- The Car Breaking Down
- Having a Cold
- What I Focus On
- What Other People Focus On
- What Other People Say
- My Reactions
- Other People's Reactions
- What Other People Do
- What I Do
- Whether I Follow the Rules
- Whether Other People Follow the Rules
- Getting Bad News

Forgiveness Takeaway

Use your results to answer the reflection questions in the following exercise.

What You Don't Control: Reflection Questions

After identifying the things you can't control, it's time to explore the energy you may be wasting on trying to control these situations so you can move toward letting go of this impulse.

Instructions

Use your results from the previous exercise to answer the following questions.

1 How many situations did you circle?

2 How often do you find yourself trying to control one or more of these situations? Which ones?

3 Are any of the situations you circled particularly frustrating for you?

4 How do you feel when you're trying to control these situations?

5 How have things turned out when you've tried to control these situations?

Forgiveness Takeaway

A big part of a forgiving mindset is understanding what you can't control and rerouting the temptation to do so. Keep this in mind the next time you feel disappointed in someone: Ask yourself if you were trying to control their actions. Is this where your disappointment stems from? The more you tune in to your own relationship with control, the more you can identify its role in hurtful situations you encounter. As you work to transform this relationship in this chapter, you will be better equipped to forgive what lies beyond your control.

Finding the Common Thread

Think back to times when you were disappointed with another person. Maybe a few weeks ago you were upset with your partner because they forgot to take out the trash. Or a friend didn't thank you for helping them move boxes into storage. Try to come up with three instances that you can recall in detail.

Instructions

Using the disappointing situations you brainstormed earlier, follow these instructions (use a separate piece of paper if needed).

1 In one to two sentences, describe what happened in each situation:

_____

_____

2 Now write down what you had expected the other person to do/say in each situation:

_____

_____

Forgiveness Takeaway

Often when you are feeling resentment, anger, or disappointment—and holding on to those emotions—it is because you expected one thing, but instead, something else happened. This is a subtle form of control many people wrestle with without even realizing it. By analyzing past disappointments and understanding what the real cause of your disappointment was in each situation, you are taking this lesson beyond theory and applying it to your own life. Going forward with this practice, you will be able to more quickly identify the source of your frustration, moving you closer to forgiving others as you recognize your role in the interaction.

But They Shouldn't Have!

Negative thoughts have endless ways of disguising themselves to sneak into your mind. Some are also harder to shake than others, and this one is possibly the hardest: "But they shouldn't have!" It's an argument that may have already come to mind as you began this chapter, and it will attempt to bind you tighter to your desire to control others if left unchecked.

Instructions

The following are some statements of everyday things people often do that they technically shouldn't. Circle the situations that have irritated you in the past.

- People should never have more than ten items in the ten items or less checkout lane.
- People should never cut others off on the freeway.
- People should never blame others for their mistakes.
- People should never be rude.
- People should never talk behind others' backs.
- People should never disrespect others.
- People should never take advantage of others.
- People should never criticize others.
- People should never cut in line.

Forgiveness Takeaway

Part of forgiveness means understanding that people are going to do things they shouldn't do—and it's not within your control. Just because someone shouldn't have done something doesn't mean they won't. You can't let this be the reason you cling to resentment. It is a game you cannot win, and it will only make you unhappy. Whenever you notice yourself thinking these four words, remind yourself of this truth: Over time, it will become easier to curb the thought before it occurs, and you'll spend a lot less time irritated with other people.

Focusing On What You Can Control

By now you have a clearer picture of the things you can't control. It's time to take the reins in your forgiveness journey by redirecting your attention to what you are able to control.

Instructions

Use your results from the previous exercises in this chapter to answer the following questions.

1 In the second exercise of this chapter, you circled all the things you don't have control over. What things didn't you circle? Write them down here.

_____

_____

2 Is there anything else you feel you have control over that wasn't on that list?

_____

Forgiveness Takeaway

Just as there is a common theme among the things you can't control (other people), there is a theme among the things you can control: you. And that's great news! It is an empowering feeling to acknowledge your control of your mood, your actions and reactions, and ultimately your ability to forgive. While you were trying to control everyone else, you were letting go of this power; now you're taking it back.

Peace Is Equanimity Meditation

When you try to control other people and situations, your response to the inevitable ups and downs and unexpected outcomes in life is to resist and hold tighter to your desired outcome. This makes it even more difficult to forgive those who have harmed you, as you ruminate on what you wish had happened and your disappointment in what actually occurred.

Equanimity teaches you to go with the ebb and flow of life—to enjoy the wins and not fall into despair when things go less favorably. It helps to reinforce your understanding of what you control and what you don't so you no longer tie your happiness to one outcome. Instead, you stay calm and centered, able to process and forgive rather than react impulsively.

Instructions

Follow these steps to complete a simple meditation for achieving and maintaining equanimity.

1 Sit in a comfortable position and close your eyes.

2 Slowly inhale and then exhale through your nose. As you breathe, say the words "Peace is equanimity" in your head.

3 Repeat step 2 for a total of one minute.

4 As you say the words, reflect on their meaning. How do you feel as you say them? What images come to mind?

Forgiveness Takeaway

Life is full of ups and downs; let this meditation be the rudder that always guides you back to a calm, forgiving center. Whenever you feel the urge to control the people or situations around you, revisit this exercise.

Responding versus Reacting

When you react, you aren't thinking about what you're doing: You're lashing out. This is where things can become blown out of proportion and people may say or do something they later regret. The opposite of reacting is where you pause and give yourself time to respond. Part of becoming more forgiving means getting familiar with the kinds of thoughts and comments you may have when you're in a reactive mode.

Instructions

Circle any of the following phrases that seem more reactive than responsive.

- I can't believe you said that.
- They're such a jerk.
- No worries, we all make mistakes.
- I need a little space right now.
- Get out of my way.
- I can't take this anymore.
- Would you please excuse me for a few minutes?

Forgiveness Takeaway

Reactive language often mirrors the degree to which you are trying to control a situation. Without realizing it, the words you are using assume control over your environment and those in it, locking you in resentment for anything that falls outside of what you planned. Recognize the language you use when you're upset with someone: Is it winding you up and making you defensive, or helping you calm down and be more forgiving?

The Punch of Disappointment

When you think something is going to happen one way, and it goes a different way, it can feel like a punch in the gut. In fact, a 2017 study by psychiatrists Alfred Kaye and David A. Ross showed that in these moments, you experience a sudden drop in dopamine (the feel-good hormone). Your brain is trying to alert you that something is wrong, even though many of the things that disappoint you are not life-threatening. Maybe you're inconvenienced or delayed, or you have to pay more than you were expecting, but your life is not in jeopardy.

Instructions

So, what do you do when you get that punched-in-the-gut feeling? Take deep breaths for sixty to ninety seconds. It sounds almost too easy, but research by psychologists Allison N. Kurti and Matthew S. Matell proves that all it takes for your dopamine levels to normalize is sixty to ninety seconds. Spend a day or so practicing this exercise: Look out for that punch in the gut—when something isn't going according to plan and you may be tempted to lash out reactively. When this happens, breathe slowly in and out for sixty to ninety seconds before responding, or you can even do the "Peace Is Equanimity Meditation" from earlier in this chapter.

Forgiveness Takeaway

In just one to two minutes, you'll feel calm, clearheaded, and able to respond to disappointment with kindness and forgiveness. You may not have control over the rest of the world, but you do have control over yourself, and this exercise is an easy way to reclaim the reins and move forward with forgiving intent.

Realistic Expectations in a World of Opposites

There are two sides to every expectation. On the one hand, you are hoping for something to happen, and on the other, you are hoping something else *doesn't* happen. This is where the struggle comes from: You are trying to control the desired outcome and keep the unwanted outcome from happening. It makes sense that you want a good outcome—who wouldn't? But it's not realistic, and it makes forgiveness more difficult. Imagine a coin being flipped: You want it to come up heads, but maybe it doesn't. You can't control what other people do or say any more than you can control that coin. Still, you might feel like you can, if only you do X or say Y. So how do you begin to let go of that belief once and for all? By resetting your expectations for reality through acknowledging the other side of the coin.

Instructions

The following are two columns of words. Each word in the left column has a corresponding opposite in the right column. Draw a line to connect each word in the left column with its opposite on the right.

Generous	Untruthful
Truthful	Mean
Responsible	Bad
Sympathetic	Unsuccessful
Kind	Insensitive
Good	Stingy
Successful	Flaky

Continued on next page

Forgiveness Takeaway

This is a simple exercise that draws your focus from desire to reality. When your expectations start to align more with the truth that there are two sides to everything—multiple possibilities beyond your control—you will save yourself frustration. Use this exercise as a jumping-off point to recognize when your expectations are getting ahead of you, and draw connections to other opposites in order to tap into a more flexible, forgiving mindset.

Expect the Unexpected Practice

To fully absorb and understand something new, you have to put it into practice. In the next few exercises, you're going to dive deeper into how to let go of control, starting with situations and events before moving on to other people (which is often the more challenging part of letting go of control).

Instructions

Before the start of your day, take a few minutes to write down what your routine for that day will look like. Fill in what your initial expectations are for each activity and how long it will take.

MY ROUTINE		
Time	**Activity**	**Expectations**
ex. 9:00 a.m.	*Drive to work*	*Light traffic; 20 minutes*
_____	_____	_____
_____	_____	_____
_____	_____	_____
_____	_____	_____
_____	_____	_____
_____	_____	_____
_____	_____	_____

As you go about your routine, note when your initial expectations don't match up with what actually happens. How does it make you feel in that moment?

Continued on next page ▶

Now, before the start of the next day, write your schedule once more—this time taking a few extra minutes to brainstorm other possibilities for what might happen within each activity. Use your experience on day 1 to help you fill in the possibilities.

MY ROUTINE

Time	Activity	Expectations	Other Possibilities
ex. 9:00 a.m.	Drive to work	Light traffic; 20 minutes	Heavy traffic; 30+ minutes

Just as you did on day 1, note when things don't go as expected. How did you feel in those moments, having considered other possibilities for what might happen?

Forgiveness Takeaway

When you open your mind to the possibilities ahead, you are better able to roll with whatever happens, rather than hanging on to expectations and feeling upset when they don't pan out. What things did you try to control during day 1 because of your focus on what "should" happen? What did you feel on day 2, when you let go of control? Keep the information and results from this activity in mind as you move on to the next exercise.

Controlling Others

Now you're going to apply the routine activity you completed in the previous exercise to other people.

Instructions

In the left-hand column of this chart, fill in different expectations you have for others that you carry with you from day to day. (Hint: Think of the things that irritate or upset you most when interacting with people. What expectations are they not meeting?)

Now spend a day (or more) noticing when people do not meet your expectations. Write these instances in the right-hand column of the chart.

INTERACTIONS WITH OTHERS

What I Expect	What Actually Happened
ex. No one should criticize me.	*Some people made critical remarks.*

Forgiveness Takeaway

You will use the information in this chart to complete the next exercise. Through this activity, you will deepen your understanding of control and how it plays into your own experiences.

Shifting Expectations

No matter how much you plan and anticipate, people have a way of surprising you. Sometimes, their response is even better than expected; other times, it leaves you feeling resentful, angry, or hurt.

Instructions

Return to your initial expectations in the previous exercise and use the following space to rewrite each one to include more possibilities for what others might or might not do. Think back to how people averted these initial expectations as you went about your day.

_____

_____

_____

_____

_____

Forgiveness Takeaway

When you reframe your expectations to account for more possibilities, you are creating a more flexible, forgiving mindset. Instead of being set on one outcome, attempting to control things to ensure success and getting angry when it doesn't happen, you are open to whatever may come your way. The more you practice this release of control, the more it will become a habit.

Continued Practice

You've spent a lot of time exploring the idea of control throughout the previous exercises—what you can and cannot control, and how to rewire the urge to control others. Because this drive is so deeply rooted in each of us, part of your forgiveness journey moving forward will include revisiting these insights and practicing the new habits you've created to keep them fresh in your mind.

Instructions

Ask yourself these questions whenever you notice controlling thoughts creeping in.

1 What am I afraid might happen if I let go of control over this person?

2 Is there any evidence to back up this outcome?

3 Is there any evidence that disputes this outcome?

4 Is there a rational way that I can make this person do or say what I want them to?

5 Is there anything concrete that *I* can do or say to encourage a good outcome?

6 What can I do or say to avoid feeling resentful or hurt if things don't work out as I'd hoped?

Forgiveness Takeaway

In this exercise, you use guiding questions to divert controlling thoughts and continue your practice of the insights gleaned in this chapter. Keep this page marked so that you can quickly return to it when you feel the urge to control anything beyond your own words or actions.

Do You Need to Set Boundaries?

One common fear you might have in letting go of attempts to control other people is that you think it means you'll become a doormat; everyone will walk all over you because you are open to possibilities outside of what you want. However, while you can't control what others do or say, you do have control over your response. And if someone does hurt you intentionally or repeatedly to a degree that affects your quality of life, you can choose to create a boundary to maintain what is best for you.

Instructions

Do you need to set up boundaries within your relationships? Answer the following questions to find out.

1 Do I find it hard to say no and avoid doing so even though it is in my best interest?

  a Yes

  b No

2 Do I always/usually give a yes or no answer immediately?

  a Yes

  b No

3 Do I struggle to communicate when I need some time to myself?

  a Yes

  b No

4 Do I avoid directly telling someone when they make me feel uncomfortable?

   a Yes

   b No

5 Do I ignore unkind comments and behaviors in order to keep the peace with someone close to me?

   a Yes

   b No

Forgiveness Takeaway

Setting boundaries is one of the kindest things you can do for yourself. In fact, according to empathy expert and author Dr. Brené Brown, the most compassionate people in the world have strong boundaries. When you allow people to ignore what is comfortable or necessary for you, you create space for resentful feelings to grow. As these negative emotions toward others build up, they expand into other relationships in your life. You are unintentionally nurturing an unforgiving mindset. The following exercises will explore the idea of boundaries in more depth.

Setting Your Boundaries

If you tended to answer yes to the questions in the previous exercise, you could benefit from setting a few boundaries within your relationships. In this exercise, you will explore what boundaries are needed and create a plan for how to establish them.

Instructions

Follow the prompts, using the lines provided.

1 What was a question that stood out to you and you answered yes to?

_____

2 Is there someone in your life who is often involved in this situation? If not, consider other questions you answered yes to that do involve someone you know.

_____

3 What might you do or say differently in this situation in order to feel more content with the interaction and your relationship with that person?

_____

4 What can they do or say differently to help you feel more content with the interaction and your relationship with them?

_____

Forgiveness Takeaway

Now that you have a clearer idea of what needs to happen in order for you to feel more secure and comfortable, you can think about communicating this to the other person. Before having a conversation, however, you can practice role-playing what you will say and how they might respond with someone you trust.

When Larger Boundaries Are Needed

In defining what your boundaries are, you may discover a relationship (or a few relationships) that cause you more harm than they offer good. The challenge here can be finding the line between normal give-and-take, and a one-sided relationship.

Instructions

Answer the following questions to identify any relationships that are more harmful than beneficial.

On these lines, name the primary people in your life—friends, family members, romantic partners, etc.

_____

_____

_____

For each of the following questions, picture your relationship with each of these people as you answer.

1 Do you typically feel energized or drained when you are with this person?
  a Energized
  b Drained

2 Do you feel you are authentically you around this person most of the time?
  a Yes
  b No

Continued on next page ▶

3 Imagine it is a good friend of yours who is in this relationship with this person. If that friend were to come to you with the facts of the relationship and ask whether they should step back from the relationship or keep this person in their life, what would you tell them?

a   Keep this person around but set some boundaries

b   Take a step back

4 If you haven't yet set boundaries, do you feel confident the person will respect them once they are established?

a   Yes

b   No

Forgiveness Takeaway

When you see the facts more objectively, it helps paint a clearer picture of how harmful or beneficial a relationship is. While you can't control another person's behavior, you can control who you choose to be around and what things you need in order to feel safe with someone. Use your results from this activity to complete the following exercise.

Saying Goodbye

If you've identified a relationship that is more harmful than beneficial, it's time to create a plan of action.

Instructions

Follow these prompts to help you move forward in doing what's right for you. Remember: The most compassionate people have strong boundaries, and sometimes these boundaries include putting space between yourself and those who repeatedly cause you harm.

1 Is it possible to allow the relationship to end naturally by not reaching out and simply declining the person's invitations?

  a Yes

  b No

  c Maybe—I'm willing to try this option first

2 If, for any reason, you don't think it's possible to simply distance yourself and allow the relationship to come to a natural end (maybe the other person just won't stop inviting you or pushing to hang out), what is the least painful way for *you* to formally end the relationship?

  a Writing a letter or email

  b Speaking in person

  c Sending a text

Continued on next page ▶

3 What are the main points of why this relationship is not healthy for you? Use your responses in the previous exercises to help you answer this question.

_____

_____

_____

Forgiveness Takeaway

Learning to end relationships that are causing you harm is an important part of your well-being—as well as a major step toward becoming a more forgiving person. Hurtful relationships encourage resentment, distrust, anger, and other emotions that hold you back from forgiving in any situation. Use your answers to this exercise to draft your letter, email, text, or in-person conversation for ending a harmful relationship.

CHAPTER 5

EVERYONE IS DOING THE BEST THEY CAN

Have you ever been cut off in traffic and thought aloud, "What a jerk"? Or maybe you are out and about when someone bumps into you, only to keep walking without so much as an apology, and you say to yourself, "How rude! They obviously don't care about anyone but themselves." Perhaps a loved one forgets a special occasion and you deem them selfish and indifferent. It's easy to assume the worst when someone has hurt you. All you know of their perspective is what you have witnessed from your own side. And as you jump to that conclusion, it becomes harder to forgive them. After all, they meant to harm you…right?

The truth is that everyone is doing the best they can. From one day to the next, we are all striving to get through our to-do lists, pay for the things we need, and find even a little joy in a hobby or quality time with loved ones. There is little room for plotting against others for the sake of it, nor is it something most desire to do. In truth, research on the subject of intent to harm proves the opposite. As psychologist Monica A. Frank outlines in "Why Are People Mean? Don't Take It Personally!" the main contributors of one person hurting another are lack of awareness, miscommunication, misdirected intentions, and self-protection—not true desire to harm. This is something you will explore more throughout this chapter and glean from your own practices in forgiveness.

Why Someone's Best May Vary

You spill coffee down your clean shirt; a fight with a loved one has you unable to focus on anything else; an unexpected challenge at home has you feeling less stable in your relationships with loved ones. Life is full of twists and turns—pressures and personal struggles—that affect everything from your mood to the people around you. And most of the time, you don't know what challenges other people are facing at a given moment. What might be going on under the surface that is making them act this way? Maybe they just found out a loved one is seriously ill, and their grief is causing them to lash out or disassociate from their surroundings. Or perhaps they simply didn't know how to communicate their feelings or are reacting out of a fear of being hurt themselves.

Every positive and negative experience—past and present—has an impact on a person's "best," which is why at one moment their best may be compassionate and thoughtful, while at another it may be irritated and distant. Sometimes, doing your best may even mean putting yourself first, with the possibility of disappointing or upsetting someone else, like ending a harmful relationship or canceling plans to recharge your batteries after a difficult day at work.

Fear and Desire

While many external influences can affect a person's best from one moment to the next, two internal influences can impact their best too: fear and desire. These emotions are deeply rooted in everyone, and when they take hold, they have a way of pushing reason and consideration for others out of view. There is an impulse tied to them that encourages reactive behavior, rather than intentional action. You will discover more about fear and desire as you work through the exercises in this chapter.

You're Doing Your Best Too

As you continue your journey through this chapter, also keep in mind that "everyone" includes you. This will be an important lesson to remember when your inner critic crops up to deal its harsh judgments. You know all too well the challenges and pressures you face, and the things you feel you need to survive and be successful. Just as a person's best can change from one day to the next, so can yours—and that is okay.

Forgiveness Made Easier

When you understand everyone is doing their best, you view them in a more positive, compassionate light than when you assume they are intentionally harming you. In fact, research by leading forgiveness researcher Everett L. Worthington Jr. shows that this outlook increases your happiness and emotional stability and also correlates to how satisfied you are with your life.

This mindset also leads to more forgiveness, as you aren't holding on to perceived slights and the idea that others are acting maliciously. Instead, you are looking at their actions with an open, empathetic heart, understanding that they themselves might be in pain, or just trying to move forward as effectively as they can. You may even seek to understand more about what is going on in their life and how you might help to alleviate what heavy emotions are weighing on them.

Rewiring Negative Assumptions

In this chapter, you'll discover over a dozen exercises designed to challenge and destroy assumptions that people are out to hurt you. Through these practices, you will shift your mindset to instead believe that everyone is doing the best they can, including you. As you train your thoughts toward this more positive perspective, you will be cultivating forgiveness along with it. Rather than grasping at the negatives in a situation, you focus on compassion—even when someone has been unkind. Are you ready for this next step in your forgiveness journey? Let's get started.

What's the Harm?

When was the last time you were disappointed with someone? Who was it, and what was the situation?

Instructions

Briefly write down the details of the situation in a couple of quick sentences, then answer the following questions.

_____

_____

1 Was there an assumption that this person wasn't trying hard enough, didn't care, or that they were doing it on purpose?

_____

2 Did that assumption lead to or fuel any existing feelings? If so, what?

_____

3 Did that assumption and any feelings that came from it make it more difficult to forgive the person?

_____

Forgiveness Takeaway

It's hard to see others as doing their best when their actions have caused you disappointment or harm. But thinking others are not doing their best actually does more harm to you: It causes you to cling to your hurt feelings, judge the other person more harshly in the future, and view the world through a negative lens. One of the most caring things you can do for yourself—and others—is to give people the benefit of the doubt. This mindset will help you let go of situations you might otherwise ruminate on, and avoid becoming resentful.

The Struggles of Others

Instructions

Here are several statements. Mark those you generally agree with as true by either circling or placing a check mark next to the word "True." Circle or otherwise mark "False" for those statements you generally don't agree with.

1 People often appear to be busy or under some kind of pressure. **True or False**

2 A stressed and overwhelmed person may have difficulty thinking rationally and/or managing their emotions. **True or False**

3 People can be really tough on themselves, leading to even more pressure. **True or False**

4 Even people who appear to have it all together can have bad days. **True or False**

5 It's hard to know what others may be struggling with internally. **True or False**

6 Even if someone is retired, or doesn't work full or part time, they can feel stress. **True or False**

Forgiveness Takeaway

If you marked most statements as true, you are likely aware to some degree that most people feel the stress of everyday life and deal with challenges that may not always be obvious to those looking in from the outside: falling behind on a big project, not having enough money to pay for a car repair, or just being pulled in too many directions. As you practice compassion by considering what might be going on in the lives of others, you loosen your grasp on anger, resentment, and disappointment, inviting forgiveness in their place.

Relate; Don't Hate

Looking through the lens of your own internal pressures and challenges—and how you respond under those conditions—is a great way to better understand where others may be coming from, and empathize with their struggles.

Instructions

Circle which answer best applies to you in each of the following questions.

1 Do you sometimes feel like with each passing year your life gets busier?

   a Yes

   b No

2 Do you sometimes feel pressure to "keep it all together"?

   a Yes

   b No

3 Have you ever been so overwhelmed that you felt as though one more disappointment—even the smallest thing—might put you over the edge?

   a Yes

   b No

4 When you're stressed or overwhelmed, do you find it difficult to think rationally and/or manage your emotions?

   a Yes

   b No

5 Do you think you are sometimes (or often) too tough on yourself?

   a Yes

   b No

6 When you've been stressed in the past, have you said or done things you later regretted?

   a Yes

   b No

7 Given all of the pressures and challenges you face in life, do you think you are doing the best you can?

   a Yes

   b No

Forgiveness Takeaway

It's so easy to get into this mindset that everyone else has it all together, and therefore the things they might do or say that hurt or upset you are intentional and personal. However, as perfect as others may like their lives to seem to you, everyone gets stressed, overtired, insecure, and more—just like you. Putting things into perspective by reflecting on your own struggles allows you to more easily tap into a compassionate response of forgiveness.

What Would Make You Feel Better?

Think of a time when you were stressed or upset, and without trying to, you let someone down. Now imagine this person knew that you were emotionally struggling, and given the circumstances, you were doing the best you could. How could they have communicated this to you in a helpful way?

Instructions

On the lines provided, write a short letter to yourself from this other person. Imagine what they would say through a compassionate response to your behavior.

_____

_____

_____

_____

_____

_____

Forgiveness Takeaway

Reflecting on the words you wrote, how might the situation have played out differently for you both if the other person reacted with compassion? You know what it feels like to inadvertently disappoint or upset someone. Instead of assuming the harm was intentional, which makes everyone feel worse, offering understanding and the benefit of the doubt keeps an unfortunate situation from escalating into something more difficult to forgive. Use this perspective to complete the following exercise.

Seeing Through a New Lens

Now that you have explored a difficult situation from your own perspective, you are going to reverse the roles.

Instructions

Think of a time when you were disappointed or angry with someone. Describe the situation on the lines provided.

_____

_____

Now remember the challenges you were dealing with in the situation you wrote about in the previous exercise, and imagine some of the struggles that person might have been experiencing when they upset you. Use this reflection to write a short letter to them on the following lines. You can refer to the letter in the previous exercise for more insight into what that person might have needed to hear.

_____

_____

_____

_____

Forgiveness Takeaway

Using personal experience is a great way to better understand another person's actions and reinforce the belief that everyone is doing the best they can. You can refer back to these exercises anytime someone upsets you in the future, to put yourself in their shoes and give a compassionate response of forgiveness.

Testing the Mindset in Real Time

You've explored the past through this mindset, and now it's time to put it to the test in the present. Gathering evidence of how it helps you to forgive and move on from upsetting situations is one of the best ways to confirm the practice for yourself. For this exercise, you'll want a small journal or pad of paper you can carry with you throughout the day.

Instructions

Spend the next day or so actively looking for situations where people bump into each other, get frustrated while waiting in line, or rush by in a panic. Every time you see a stressful situation play out—or are involved in the situation yourself—note it in your journal or pad of paper, then write, "Everyone is doing the best they can." You can also say the words out loud as you write them to really bring home the message.

Bonus: In preparation of this exercise, you can post sticky notes with "Everyone is doing the best they can" written on them in places where you will see them regularly (the bathroom mirror, in your car, on your computer, etc.).

Forgiveness Takeaway

Going out into the world and practicing this mindset firsthand is the first step in tearing down those old neural pathways associated with people not doing their best and laying down new ones that are positive and compassionate. Use your results from this exercise to complete the following exercise.

How Does It Feel to See Others As Doing Their Best?

Empathy expert and author Dr. Brené Brown says, "I know my life is better when I work from the assumption that everyone is doing the best they can." The person who gains the most from seeing others as doing their best is you, as you will explore more in this exercise.

Instructions

Using your results from the previous exercise, answer the questions that follow.

1 How did you feel as you set off on your day with the intention of seeing people as doing their best?

2 Were you able to look beyond people's outer actions and explore the internal struggles they might be facing?

3 Did you feel more compassion toward people who were complaining or being rude, knowing they were doing their best?

4 How did you feel as the day came to an end?

Forgiveness Takeaway

When you set off with the mindset that others are doing their best, you are able to respond more compassionately to their behavior and let go of negative experiences much easier. Of course, this mindset is one you will want to keep practicing in order for it to stick, so complete the previous exercise and answer these reflection questions more than once.

Everyone Is Doing the Best They Can Meditation

One of the benefits of meditation is that because your mind is in a relaxed state, it's very impressionable—much like hypnosis. This is the perfect space for reinforcing the mindset that everyone is doing their best.

Instructions

Just like the previous meditations in this workbook, this meditation is paired with a mantra. In this case, your mantra is "Everyone is doing the best they can." Follow these steps to complete the meditation.

1 Find a quiet, comfortable place to sit.

2 Slowly inhale and then exhale through your nose. As you inhale and exhale, say the words "Everyone is doing the best they can" in your head.

3 Repeat step 2 for a total of one minute. Notice how you feel as you say the words and breathe.

Forgiveness Takeaway

This meditation takes only a few minutes to do but is so effective in rewiring your neural pathways to allow this forgiving mindset to take root. Whenever you are faced with a particularly challenging situation that has you struggling to feel compassion for someone else, revisit this meditation for a little boost.

It's Not Personal

For many, a big obstacle to believing others are doing their best is that things can feel so personal. After all, that hurtful comment was directed at *you*. That person's actions hurt *you*. The key to fully accepting this belief will be understanding that things are rarely personal.

Instructions

Answer the following questions.

1 Look back at the "Random Acts of Forgiveness" exercise in Chapter 3: Did the altercations you had with other people seem more or less random?

 a Mostly intentional

 b Mostly random

2 Do these types of altercations happen more or less regularly in your daily life?

 a Regularly

 b Infrequently

 c There are periods where it seems regular and periods where it seems infrequent

3 Which of the following have you felt in the last two weeks? Circle all that apply.

 a Insulted

 b Ignored

 c Judged

 d Delayed

 e Blamed

 f _____ (add your own)

 g _____ (add your own)

Continued on next page ▶

Using the lines provided, reflect on any times when you may have made someone else feel something you circled in the previous question:

_____

_____

_____

_____

How often were these instances personal? How often were they a result of your own inner challenges or misunderstandings?

_____

_____

_____

_____

Forgiveness Takeaway

When something frustrating or disappointing happens, it can feel so personal, yet when you step back to reflect on things as a whole, it's often random—and rarely as personal as you might think. The following exercises will explore this theory in more depth.

Flipping the Script

Not taking what others do or say personally can be a real challenge for many. That's why this exercise is going to make it a little easier by turning the tables to look at your own behavior.

Instructions

Read the following statements. Mark those you generally agree with as true by either circling or placing a check mark next to the word "True." Circle or otherwise mark "False" for those statements you generally don't agree with.

1 Sometimes I wake up feeling irritable or down. **True or False**

2 I'm not always kind or attentive to other people when I am in a bad mood. **True or False**

3 When I'm feeling stressed or overwhelmed, I'm more likely to snap at someone. **True or False**

4 When I'm in a hurry, I pay less attention to the people around me. **True or False**

Forgiveness Takeaway

Everyone experiences bad moods that cause them to act out against others. It's a by-product, and it's not personal. Use the phrases you marked as true as mantras during those moments when it feels challenging to believe others are doing their best and their actions aren't personal.

Has It Happened to Others?

One main part of taking things personally is the feeling that the negative situation you're dealing with is only happening to you—that you've been singled out for this unique experience. Perhaps a friend you thought you were close to hasn't been prioritizing your friendship lately, forgetting plans or canceling at the last minute. Or a coworker made an unnecessary, critical comment that still stings. In this exercise, you'll challenge the belief that it is only happening to you.

Instructions

Pick at least three people close to you whom you can have an honest, open conversation with about personal experiences. In each conversation, ask them the following.

1 Have you ever been criticized for something?

2 Have you ever felt stressed at work?

3 Have you ever been cut off while driving?

4 Have you ever cut someone off while driving?

5 Has someone ever canceled plans with you at the last minute?

6 Have you ever canceled plans with someone at the last minute?

7 Have you ever felt disappointed by someone?

8 Have you ever disappointed someone?

Forgiveness Takeaway

Affirming that everyone experiences many of the same situations is a great way to see for yourself that many things aren't as personal as they may have felt in the moment. When you know this to be true, it is easier to let go of these situations and forgive the other person, understanding that they were doing their best and it likely wasn't intentional.

Exploring Self-Compassion

While it's been helpful to use your own life as evidence for others doing their best, it's also important that you see how you are doing your best too. Remember, forgiveness isn't just something you give to others: Sometimes you will also need to practice forgiving yourself. The first step will be recognizing when you are being hard on yourself. For this exercise, you will want to have a small journal or pad of paper on hand.

Instructions

For the next day or so, write down every self-critical thought you catch yourself having. Unsure of what counts? Here are some examples of self-critical thoughts:

- Why did I do that? That was so dumb.
- Why aren't I as smart as them?
- I can't believe I said something so awkward!

Forgiveness Takeaway

It can be jarring to see how often we criticize ourselves—and how mean we can be in these comments. How do you feel when you reflect on the self-talk you wrote down? Would you say these things to someone you loved, like a good friend or significant other? Probably not. Calling attention to these criticisms and seeing them objectively after the fact can even be the push some people need to start being kinder to themselves. However, the next exercise will give you more guidance in practicing self-compassion.

Seeing Yourself As Doing Your Best

In previous exercises, you practiced seeing others as doing their best. Here, you are going to use the same technique to see yourself as doing your best.

Instructions

First, get yourself into the mindset the night before you complete this exercise by posting sticky notes in places where you will see them the next day. The notes should read, "You're doing the best you can."

Then review your self-criticisms from the previous exercise: These are the types of comments you will be looking for as you do this exercise.

Now spend an entire day watching for moments when negative self-talk creeps in, and address it by repeating the phrase "You're doing the best you can" in your head (or out loud, if you prefer). You can even start the phrase with your first name, or an endearing nickname for yourself—whatever someone close to you would say if it were them telling you that you're doing the best you can.

Forgiveness Takeaway

How did you feel going into the day with this mindset? How did you feel at the end of the day? It's amazing how these simple words can positively change the way you see yourself and help you forgive and move on from your mistakes. In fact, when you speak to yourself with care, you naturally reduce your negative self-talk rate over time. Continue to practice this exercise to make self-compassion—and self-forgiveness—a habit.

Forgiving Fear and Desire

In previous exercises, you explored the external forces that can impact a person's best (including your own), such as a stressful day at work or an argument with a loved one. There are also two key internal forces that can impact someone's best: fear and desire. These hugely motivating mind states can push you to do things you might not otherwise have done, including harming someone. In the exercises that follow, you will explore the role fear and desire can play in your choices and the choices of others.

Instructions

Read the following statements. Mark those you generally agree with as true by either circling or placing a check mark next to the word "True." Circle or otherwise mark "False" for those statements you generally don't agree with.

1 Sometimes the desire to be right feels so strong that I have trouble listening to the other side of an argument. **True or False**

2 Sometimes the fear of looking foolish stops me from admitting when I've made a mistake. **True or False**

3 Sometimes the fear of being excluded can cause me to be upset if someone doesn't return my call or text right away. **True or False**

4 Sometimes the desire to have something is so strong that I ignore what other people involved in the situation may want. **True or False**

5 Sometimes the fear of being late causes me to be short with or even rude to another person. **True or False**

6 Sometimes the desire to feel or seem successful has led me to take more credit (or feel tempted to take more credit) for something than perhaps I should. **True or False**

Continued on next page ▶

With these situations in mind, can you think of other scenarios where you might have caused harm to someone because you were acting out of fear or desire? Write your reflections on the lines provided.

_____

_____

_____

_____

_____

Forgiveness Takeaway

Fear and desire are two often underlying culprits for why someone may cause you harm, despite doing the best they can. Of course, this is easier to understand when you look through the lens of your own experiences with fear and desire, which is why this exercise focuses on common ways many of us may hurt someone, or negatively impacted our relationship with them, due to being afraid or focused on our own wants. Knowing this helps you when it comes to forgiving other people (and yourself), because you understand what may have driven the behavior—and can relate to their mistake.

Asking for Forgiveness Practice

As you reflect on your own mistakes, you may begin to notice guilt or anger toward yourself sprouting up. In this exercise, you will take steps to release these heavy emotions by asking for forgiveness from those you may have harmed when fear or desire took over. These conversations can feel difficult at first, which is why this exercise will serve as practice before you begin a real dialogue with someone you have harmed.

Instructions

In the space provided, write a short note to a few people you have harmed in the past. Begin by apologizing, and then explain why you did what you did, within the context of fear or desire. End your note with the words "Please forgive me," or another phrase that you would use to ask for forgiveness.

Dear _____,

_____

_____

_____

Dear _____,

_____

_____

_____

Continued on next page ▶

Dear _____,

_____

_____

_____

Are there any other people you would like forgiveness from? Write your notes to them on a separate piece of paper. (Remember these notes are practice, so you won't send them to that person.)

Forgiveness Takeaway

In each instance in this exercise, you have reflected more on how fear or desire drove your behavior, understanding that you never intended to hurt the other person. You were doing the best you could. When you can see how easily fear and desire take over your own actions, it becomes easier to see it in others and forgive them for their mistakes.

But before you jump into forgiving others, you will let go of your own past mistakes by seeking forgiveness from yourself. Use your forgiveness notes to complete the following exercise.

Asking for Forgiveness Without Training Wheels

Sometimes your best hurts people, and while fear and desire can lead you to act in ways you might not otherwise, it is important to ask for forgiveness for these mistakes. Not only will it ease your own guilt and anger toward yourself, but it will also allow you both to move forward in positivity.

Instructions

Choose at least one person from your notes in the previous exercise to ask forgiveness from, and use the prompts that follow to plan how you will open this dialogue and what you will say. (Keep in mind that you do not need to mention fear or desire, or any part of why you behaved the way you did—that's not part of the apology. It's part of the understanding for yourself.)

1 Who are you reaching out to?

_____

2 How will you contact them (over the phone, through a written letter, in person, etc.)?

_____

3 When will you be reaching out to them? If not right now, set a specific date and time, write it down here, and put it on your calendar so you will remember.

_____

Continued on next page ▶

You can use the rest of this space, or a separate piece of paper, to outline what you will say, or write your full monologue or letter.

_____

_____

_____

_____

_____

_____

Forgiveness Takeaway

Asking forgiveness is a critical step in being able to forgive others. It
reminds you that you have made mistakes, disappointed others, or caused
harm too. It doesn't mean you're a bad person: You are doing your best,
and sometimes things happen.

Are Your Reasons Their Reasons?

Now that you've explored how fear and desire have impacted your choices, let's take a closer look at how they may have led others to disappoint you or cause you harm.

Instructions

Fill out the following chart with at least three situations where someone disappointed or hurt you in the past. Use the column on the right to reflect on how fear or desire may have contributed to what happened.

Their Name	What Happened	Fear or Desire?
_____	_____	_____
_____	_____	_____
_____	_____	_____
_____	_____	_____
_____	_____	_____
_____	_____	_____

Forgiveness Takeaway

Just as your own fear or desire can negatively impact those around you, others can be swayed by these driving forces too. Again, it doesn't mean they are bad people: They are doing their best to get by. Use this exercise to forgive past hurt, and maintain a forgiving mindset as you continue your journey.

Giving Forgiveness Practice

To further bridge the gap between your mistakes and the mistakes made by others, you will write notes of forgiveness to people who have harmed you.

Instructions

In the space provided, write a short note to a few people who have hurt you in the past. Explain that you understand they were just doing their best, and consider whether their actions were driven by fear or desire.

Dear _____,

_____

_____

_____

Dear _____,

_____

_____

_____

Dear _____,

_____

_____

_____

Forgiveness Takeaway

Few set out to harm, but it can happen when those instinctive fears or desires take hold. Use these notes to complete the following exercise.

Giving Forgiveness Without Training Wheels

Once you've practiced giving forgiveness, it is time to put your efforts into action. Your notes from the previous exercise will be your guide through this experience.

Instructions

Choose at least one person from your notes to give forgiveness to, and use the prompts that follow to plan how you will open this dialogue and what you will say. (Once again, keep in mind that you do not need to mention fear or desire, or any part of why you understand their behavior—that's not part of giving them forgiveness; it's part of the understanding for yourself.)

1 Who are you reaching out to?

   _____

2 How will you contact them (over the phone, through a written letter, in person, etc.)?

   _____

3 When will you be reaching out to them? If not right now, set a specific date and time, write it down here, and put it on your calendar so you will remember.

   _____

Continued on next page ▶

You can use the rest of this space, or a separate piece of paper, to outline what you will say, or write your full monologue or letter.

_____

_____

_____

_____

_____

_____

Forgiveness Takeaway

As you've uncovered in previous chapters, forgiveness is a powerful gift. Not only are you releasing the weight of your disappointment, resentment, or anger, but you are also easing the pain of the person you're forgiving. After all, just as it can be difficult for you to recognize that you are doing your best—and forgive yourself when your best varies from one day to the next—it is difficult for others as well. We are our own worst critics.

The Best Response

While seeing everyone as doing the best they can helps you to respond with compassion and forgiveness, not every situation is identical. Sometimes the compassionate response is to be gentle, while sometimes it requires being firmer. These types of compassionate responses are characterized as the following:

- Gentle: Passive stance, soft tone
- Firm: Strong stance, assertive tone

A gentle response can be best in smaller, less hurtful encounters, like when the barista messes up your coffee order, or someone bumps into you on the sidewalk. More harmful situations, like when a friend uses biting comments to intentionally hurt your feelings, may require a firmer response. Part of your forgiveness journey will be identifying which response is best in a given situation.

Instructions

The following are scenarios that offer an opportunity to forgive. Mark whether you believe your compassionate response should be gentle or firm.

1 A friend has texted you at the last minute to cancel plans. You remember her saying something earlier that week about a big work deadline she had coming up. What is the best response?
   a Gentle
   b Firm

2 Someone bumped into you on the sidewalk while looking at their phone. What is the best response?
   a Gentle
   b Firm

Continued on next page ▶

3 Someone is physically or emotionally harming you or another person. What is the best response?

   a Gentle

   b Firm

4 Someone is speaking to you rudely. What is the best response?

   a Gentle

   b Firm

Answer Key:

1 a   **2** a   **3** b   **4** b

Forgiveness Takeaway

Compassion is often thought of as gentle, but it can also be given in a firm way. Use the results of this exercise to identify which response is best in the situations you encounter going forward.

Forgiving Yourself for Not Being Ready to Forgive

There may be times during your journey when you're just not ready to forgive, and that's okay. Even when you understand the reasons for why someone might have acted the way they did, sometimes the wound is too new and intense to give forgiveness.

Instructions

When you are feeling clearheaded and forgiving, use the lines provided to write a letter to yourself for a time in the future when you may not be ready to forgive someone. Forgive yourself for this, and remind yourself that this is okay: You may forgive them eventually, or you may not. Forgiveness doesn't always need to be directed at someone else.

Dear _____,

_____

_____

_____

_____

_____

Sincerely,

_____

Forgiveness Takeaway

In forgiving yourself for being unable to forgive someone else, you are still practicing forgiveness. This is an incredibly self-compassionate act that offers healing when pain is fresh. Read your letter whenever you feel unready to forgive.

3

CONTINUING YOUR FORGIVENESS JOURNEY

You may be nearing the end of this workbook, but your forgiveness journey isn't coming to a close. Each new day will bring more opportunities to heal, offer kindness, and connect with those around you through forgiveness. You may also encounter different challenges in the future that encourage you to test your skills and expand on lessons you've learned in your journey so far. It will also be important as you move forward to remember the time and effort you have already put in, and the insights and tips that will serve you in later situations.

This part will give you the tools to continue on your journey long after you have read these pages. It will also provide the space and guidance to reflect on how far you have come so you can maintain your progress. Chapter 6 begins with an exploration of the connection between gratitude and nurturing the forgiving mindset you've worked toward throughout Parts 1 and 2 of this workbook. After looking back on your journey so far, and savoring your triumphs, you will discover practices for continuing your growth in being a forgiving person. It's time to take the next step in forgiveness. Let's get started.

YOUR FORGIVING PRESENT AND FUTURE

Congratulations! You made the decision to journey toward a more forgiving you and worked through dozens of exercises along the way. At every step, and through every obstacle, you've learned new insights into forgiveness, from why it's important to forgive to what has made forgiving a challenge in your own experiences. Your heart has invited in more compassion for others and yourself, and you've trained your thoughts toward positivity. What you've accomplished is pretty remarkable—and it's worth celebrating.

It's time to savor all the goodness you have gained from your journey thus far. What have you given to other people? What have you given to yourself? As experts at Harvard Business School outlined in a 2016 study, this kind of reflection helps you connect more meaning to your experiences, gain new insights, and ensure what you've gained stays with you as you continue forward in forgiveness.

The Path Ahead

Of course, your journey is not over. Just like a healthy diet or relationships with loved ones, forgiveness is a lifestyle routine that is always in progress. If you had been working out at a gym and upon reaching your ideal weight you suddenly stopped working out, what would happen? All of your fitness gains would eventually be lost. Forgiveness is similar; to maintain a forgiving mindset and build upon your skills, you will need to continue practicing.

Reinforcing Your Progress

Continued practice in forgiveness is especially important because it is still a new, impressionable belief.

Every time someone harmed you in the past and you held on to hurt feelings, believing it was an intentional act of malice, you were activating and strengthening a neural pathway in your brain that connects forgiveness to challenge, frustration, and doubts about whether the effort is worth it. As outlined in a study titled "Sources of the Continued Influence Effect: When Misinformation in Memory Affects Later Inferences," by psychologists Hollyn Johnson and Colleen Seifert, a neural pathway such as this, once created, becomes a guide for how you think about and interpret certain situations. And over years of negative assumptions and struggling to let go of past experiences, this resentful, discouraged pathway is pretty strong.

So, while you have been tearing down old beliefs and building new ones throughout the exercises in this workbook, those fresh, forgiving neural pathways are less ingrained in your brain. Left uncultivated, they aren't as stable against a challenging situation in the future. Not only that, but those old beliefs can resurface like weeds in their place. Through continued practice, you will strengthen the forgiving pathways you have developed throughout this workbook.

A More Forgiving You

In the following exercises, you will be doing a lot of reflecting on everything you've gained so far in your forgiveness journey. The first three exercises will tap into the powerful effects of gratitude to strengthen the connection of forgiveness to your overall well-being. Then you'll complete a second practice in savoring the goodness, further nourishing this connection. As you move deeper into the chapter, you'll explore practices for building on the skills you've cultivated and continuing forgiveness in the future. "Preparing for Bumps in the Road" will help you pinpoint which areas of forgiveness you may need to focus on in order to strengthen your skills. In one of the final exercises, you'll write a letter to your future self, reminding yourself of why this journey is so important and setting up a plan of action to stay motivated through possible challenges.

Remember that your journey is not ending: Forgiveness is a way of life that you will continue to hone over time and experience. You can also return to this workbook whenever you want to recollect different insights and tips and redo exercises with current challenges in mind. You have come a long way in forgiveness, and your success does not stop here. Keep reading to discover more insights and tips to help you along the way.

Gratitude for What You've Put Into This Journey

You've given time and energy to this workbook, and that's something worth celebrating in and of itself. It's time to reflect on what you've put into your forgiveness journey and acknowledge your efforts.

Instructions

Answer the following questions using your experiences from this workbook.

1 How much time do you think you've spent on this workbook thus far? Think back to each chapter and the exercises you completed, and give an estimate: _____ (hours/minutes)

2 Did you spend any extra time outside of the exercises practicing or reflecting on forgiveness? If so, estimate that time: _____ (hours/minutes)

Think of all the different things you might have been doing (watching TV, reading a book, etc.) instead of completing this workbook: What did you give up to make time for this journey?

_____

_____

Forgiveness Takeaway

It's important to recognize all the time and effort you put in, as well as what you gave up, to be a more forgiving person. You made this a priority for yourself, and there were choices involved—choices that may have been challenging at times. When you've worked hard for something, you value it more—and the more you value something, the more you will nurture it moving forward. This exercise will help you stay motivated in continuing your forgiveness journey.

Gratitude for What You've Given to Others

You've spent a lot of time giving forgiveness to others, and that is a wonderful gift. Here, you are going to take a few minutes to recognize the impact your forgiveness journey has had on other people.

Instructions

Take a few moments to remember how much forgiving you've been doing through this workbook.

1 How many people do you estimate you gave forgiveness to? Include any times you gave forgiveness while doing the practical exercises, as well as any times you were giving it outside of the workbook as you were becoming a more forgiving person. _____

2 How many people did you ask forgiveness from? _____

3 How many times did you forgive yourself? _____

4 Totaling up all of your efforts, how many people did you have a forgiveness interaction with (including yourself)? _____

Forgiveness Takeaway

You have touched lives with forgiveness, relieving others and yourself of emotional burdens. Take a few moments to reflect on your impact. Whenever you feel doubts creeping in about whether forgiveness is worth it, or you're faced with a more challenging situation you are tempted to give up on, return to this exercise to remember just how many lives you have touched through forgiving thus far.

Gratitude for Each Person You Forgave

Now that you've explored what you've given to others, it's time to further embed the positive associations of each forgiveness practice by zooming in on each experience in a bit more detail. Here, you will look back at the different people you have forgiven during your journey.

Instructions

Use the lines provided to reflect on each individual you forgave during your journey. What were their names (or identifiers, e.g., "woman on subway," if they were strangers)?

_____

_____

_____

_____

_____

Forgiveness Takeaway

The raw numbers may have been eye-opening to see in the previous exercise, but when you add a name to each instance, the real significance of your actions is clear. For every person's name you wrote here, you made a positive difference—in their lives and yours. Remember this as you continue your journey: There may be challenging situations ahead, but the rewards are worth working for!

Taking In the Goodness, Part 2

You started out this chapter reflecting on just how much time and effort you've put into this practice—acknowledging the value of your hard work and how many people you've helped. Now you'll continue savoring the goodness by reflecting on some of the specific practices you did and how they made you feel. Just like you did in the Chapter 3 exercise "Taking In the Goodness," you're going to recount these positive experiences in detail to embed them more deeply into your nervous system, strengthening that motivation-reward pathway.

Instructions

To help you relive some of the highs from your forgiveness practices, write down two to three words on the lines provided to describe how each moment felt.

1 When you were practicing the gift of forgiveness, how did you feel after the very first interaction when you were able to put someone else's mind at ease? _____, _____, and _____.

2 When you recognized you were trying to control another person's behavior and let go of that attempt, how did it feel? _____, _____, and _____.

3 What did it feel like the first time you used one of the exercises for rebalancing your nervous system ("You're Safe: A Self-Compassion Meditation," "4-7-8 Breathing") to reduce stress? _____, _____, and _____.

4 What did it feel like to forgive yourself? _____, _____, and _____.

5 How did it feel the first time you saw someone acting out angrily and recognized they were doing the best they could? _____, _____, and _____.

6 The first time you had an opportunity to place your hand on your heart and say the words "I forgive, I forgive, I forgive," how did you feel? _____, _____, and _____.

7 When you first did the "Loving-Kindness Meditation" exercise, how did you feel afterward? _____, _____, and _____.

Forgiveness Takeaway

By connecting how good you felt to the details of each experience, you are reinforcing those forgiving behaviors. This reinforcement will help you stay the course as you continue on your forgiveness journey.

How Has This Practice Healed Your Heart?

You've been on quite a journey since starting this workbook. And all the while you've been practicing forgiveness, your heart has been healing from any anger, resentment, disappointment, or hurt that had previously taken up residence there. Now that you are coming to the end of this workbook, it's time to reflect on how your heart has healed.

Instructions

Look back at the people you have worked to forgive through these exercises. On the lines provided, describe how you felt toward them and what they had done before you started this workbook. Then describe how you are feeling now.

_____

_____

_____

_____

_____

Forgiveness Takeaway

Exploring how these practices have healed your heart—or started the mending process—is a testament to the power of forgiveness. Even if you have not fully forgiven someone, the seeds of compassion have been sown, and you are closer to healing than when you first started your journey.

How Has This Practice Opened Your Heart?

Now that you've explored how forgiveness has healed your heart from past pain or anger, let's look at how it has opened your heart to a forgiving future.

Instructions

Answer the following questions on the lines provided.

1　When you saw someone acting out in anger or frustration before you completed this workbook, what did you think or feel?

_____

_____

2　When you imagine someone acting out in anger or frustration in the future, what do you think or feel now?

_____

_____

3　How have you offered compassion to others through different exercises in this workbook? Do you think this practice has helped you to be kinder to other people and yourself?

_____

_____

Continued on next page ▶

4 How have you offered compassion to yourself through different exercises in this workbook?

_____

_____

5 How will you continue to offer compassion beyond this workbook? Are there any exercises you will return to, either to complete them again or recall different tricks or insights?

_____

_____

Forgiveness Takeaway

This is one of the biggest benefits of forgiveness: an open heart filled with compassion. Your answers in this exercise will help you keep your heart open—and perhaps open it even more—as you continue your forgiveness journey.

What Have You Lost?

In Chapter 1, you considered what you might lose by becoming more forgiving. Now that you have been traveling along on your forgiveness journey for a while, what *have* you lost?

Instructions

Circle the things you have begun to let go of as you've become more forgiving. You can also add your own options to this list.

- Resentment
- Anger
- Sympathy
- Isolation
- Confidence

- Bitterness
- Kindness
- Sadness
- Anxiety
- Wisdom

- Judgment
- Vengeance
- Strength
- Stress

How does it feel as you look back on what you have lost?

_____

Forgiveness Takeaway

This exercise is a tangible reminder of not only the heavy emotions you have released through forgiving, but also why it is important to continue on your forgiveness journey. You've done the work before, and you have the power to keep it up, no matter the challenges life may throw your way!

What Have You Gained?

In the previous exercise, you explored the mind states you've lost or reduced along your forgiveness journey. But what have you gained?

Instructions

Circle the things you have gained as you've become more forgiving. You can also add your own options to this list.

- Wisdom
- Joy
- Ignorance
- Stress
- Flexibility
- Stronger relationships

- Patience
- Fear
- Freedom
- Energy
- Bitterness
- Compassion

- Strength
- Confidence
- Anger
- Power

How does it feel as you look back at what you've gained?

Forgiveness Takeaway

This is the multiplier effect of forgiveness: By taking on one good habit, you have also taken on other positive traits and practices. Wisdom, power, flexibility, compassion—these are a part of forgiveness. And now they are a part of you. Return to this exercise whenever you feel doubtful of how far you have come, or if you are faced with a more challenging situation.

What Are You Most Proud Of?

You covered a lot in this workbook, and every lesson, practice, and challenge has helped you to be more forgiving.

Instructions

Take a few moments to reflect, then write about what moments stand out to you from your experience with this workbook. What makes you feel proud?

_____

_____

_____

_____

_____

Forgiveness Takeaway

You've earned this moment of recognition! Not to mention that every time you savor a good feeling, you strengthen those neural connections in your brain—encouraging you to keep up the forgiving behavior. Drink it all in.

Preparing for Bumps in the Road

Everyone has strengths and weaknesses, and it is no different when it comes to forgiveness. Depending on your own forgiveness strengths and weaknesses, there may be times in your journey when it feels more difficult to forgive. The first step in overcoming these obstacles is identifying where there is room for improvement.

Instructions

Circle any statements that resonate with you. You can also add anything that is not listed here but that you feel you need to work on as you continue your journey.

- I have a hard time saying no to people.
- There is still a relationship (or relationships) in my life that cause more harm than good.
- I sometimes find it difficult to see others as doing their best.
- Even though I know the only thing I control is my response, sometimes I still instinctively try to control others.
- I have a hard time seeing myself as doing my best when I make mistakes.
- Sometimes I still want to hang on to my anger.
- I'm still holding on to a feeling of resentment toward someone else.

Bookmark the chapter exercises that focus on each challenge you circled.

Forgiveness Takeaway

When you know the areas in which you can improve your forgiveness skills, you can prioritize practices that strengthen those skills. This will set you up for success in the future.

What Being a More Forgiving Person Means to You

Throughout this workbook, you've explored how it feels to give forgiveness and to ask for it. You've experienced firsthand how forgiving changes your life and relationships. Now let's reflect on these changes.

Instructions

On the lines provided, write what you believe it means to be a more forgiving person, based on your journey thus far. Think about how you feel now compared to before you started this workbook, what you've learned, and how your interactions with others may have evolved.

_____

_____

_____

_____

_____

Forgiveness Takeaway

This has been an incredible journey through your inner world and the world around you—and it's not over! There is profound meaning in both what you've discovered and what you've accomplished. Use this exercise to reflect on these lessons and successes, and remind yourself of why you are on this journey.

Your Favorite Practices

You've done a lot of different exercises on the path to becoming more forgiving. Which ones did you find most helpful? Enjoyable?

Instructions

Use the lines provided to list your favorite exercises from this workbook.

_____

_____

_____

From your list of favorite exercises, which ones are you committed to practicing going forward? Write the exercise name, as well as how regularly you aim to practice that exercise.

_____

_____

_____

Forgiveness Takeaway

It's important to keep up your practices in forgiveness to maintain an open and compassionate heart. Keep your workbook in a place where you'll see it regularly so you can easily return to different practices and insights as you continue your journey. You can even schedule times for one or more of your favorite exercises in your phone or desktop calendar.

A Partner in Forgiveness

Although many people have been involved in your forgiveness journey, for the most part this came from the work you were doing on your own. However, it's so helpful to have someone you can call when you're struggling to let go of something someone said or did. A forgiveness buddy, someone who can help steer you back in the right direction, is a priceless gift and a powerful commitment to your journey. This person can also complete the exercises in this workbook to begin their own journey, and they can refer to different lessons and tricks when you need a little help (and vice versa).

Instructions

Choose your partner in forgiveness, and set a plan of action for sticking to the buddy system throughout your journey. Questions to discuss with your partner include the following:

1 How often will you check in with each other?

2 What method of communication is best for check-ins and asking for advice (email, phone, in person, etc.)?

3 What specific goals or areas of improvement are each of you looking to focus on in your forgiveness journeys going forward?

Forgiveness Takeaway

A partner in forgiveness can be just what you need to stick to your goals—and have more fun along the way. Be sure to communicate what you are hoping to get out of this arrangement, and how often you hope to check in with each other, vent, or ask for advice.

Dear Future You

In Chapter 1, you wrote a letter to your past self. Now that you've completed the exercises in this workbook, you're going to write a letter to your *future* self—reminding you of what you've discovered and how far you've come.

Instructions

On a separate piece of paper, write a letter to your future self. Include details about your forgiveness journey so far—from your challenges to your triumphs—and what your hopes are for where you will be when you are reading the letter later on. Also, be sure to offer any encouraging words you think you might need to hear if you are faced with a difficult situation or feel tempted to hold on to hurtful feelings.

When you are done writing, seal the letter in an envelope addressed to yourself and date it to be opened sometime in the future. Whether this is three months from now, a year from now, or even longer is up to you.

Forgiveness Takeaway

A letter addressed to you, from you, is a powerful tool—no one knows you better than you do. Later, when you have forgotten your words and this workbook may be less fresh in your mind, it will be time to open the letter and receive the wisdom and support to keep you practicing forgiveness. You can even save it for a time when you are really struggling to forgive someone.

Sharing Forgiveness

As you've moved through the exercises in this workbook, you've uncovered more and more about how forgiveness heals both you and others, and allows you to keep an open mind in challenging situations. And now that you have the tools to forgive, you can share those tools with someone else.

Instructions

Choose someone to share what you've learned, from the benefits of forgiveness to the different theories and practices for becoming a more forgiving person. This can be anyone, from a family member to a friend to a significant other or even coworker. You can use the following space to outline what you will talk about.

Forgiveness Takeaway

It feels good to help someone else let go of emotional burdens and move forward with a positive mindset. It also helps you keep everything you've learned fresh in your mind as you continue your own forgiveness journey.

Forgiveness Assessment

At the beginning of this workbook, you completed a forgiveness assessment to see how forgiving you were at the start of your journey. It's time to revisit this exercise to see where you are now.

Instructions

Read the following statements. Give yourself a score of 1–5 based on how much each statement resonates with you.

> 5 = I agree very strongly with this statement
> 4 = I agree with this statement
> 3 = I somewhat agree with this statement
> 2 = I don't really agree with this statement
> 1 = I don't agree at all with this statement

1 If someone is late to meet you, you assume they don't value your time. ___

2 If someone interrupts you while you're talking, you immediately feel annoyed with them. ___

3 If someone disappoints you, it's hard to let it go and move on. ___

4 If someone has let you down, you're not sure how to address it in a calm and effective way. ___

5 If someone cuts you off while driving, you assume they are a jerk.

___

6 If someone doesn't call or text you back right away, you feel ignored and irritated. ___

7 When you do something for someone else, and they don't help you in return, you get angry with them. ___

8 If someone has an opinion that contradicts yours, you get defensive and think negatively toward that person. ___

Total Your Score: [ ]

Forgiveness Takeaway

With a range of 8–40 points, the lower your score, the more forgiving you are. How does your score here compare to your score in the initial assessment? Use the results from this exercise to discover how far you have come in forgiving, or what aspects of forgiveness you want to improve on in the future. Remember, your journey isn't over: Each day brings new opportunities to learn, heal, and flourish as a more forgiving person.

ABOUT THE AUTHOR

Meredith Hooke, founder of ZenSmarts, is a certified meditation and mindfulness instructor and life coach who teaches others how to find peace of mind via workshops in the US and abroad. She has spent more than twenty years studying Eastern philosophies, attending intensive meditation retreats, and researching how our minds and brains work. She has been featured on *Tiny Buddha*, *Thrive Global*, and *A Daring Adventure*. Visit her at ZenSmarts.com.